Anger:
Let the Tiger Out,
But Keep It on a Leash

Anger:
Let the Tiger Out,
But Keep It on a Leash

Mary Ellen Halloran, MFT

Timepiece Publishing Company
Personal Development Books and CDs

Anger: Let the Tiger Out, But Keep It on a Leash

By Mary Ellen Halloran, MFT

Timepiece Publishing Company
Post Office Box 3508
Oakland, CA 94609 U.S.A.

http://www.timepiecepublishing.com

Printed in the United States of America

Editing and layout: Susan Ferguson
Cover design and illustrations: Valerie Knight
Printing: United Graphics, Inc.

Publisher's Cataloging-in-Publication
Halloran, Mary Ellen.
Anger : let the tiger out but keep it on a leash /Mary Ellen Halloran.
p. cm.
Includes bibliographical references and index.
LCCN 2006907094
ISBN-13: 978-0-9788192-0-0
1. Anger.   I. Title.
BF575.A5H35   2007   152.4'7
QBI06-600548

Table of Contents

Illustrations

Acknowledgements

Many people have had a hand in the creation of this book, some indirectly and others more directly. First, I acknowledge those who may not even be aware of the significance of their contributions: my teachers at the California Institute of Integral Studies, who inspired me to achieve my goal of becoming a therapist; my supervisors at traineeships and internships, especially Wilma Bass and Elizabeth Schenk, who taught me how to listen compassionately; my consultants, especially David Akullian, Joyce Cunningham and Jeff Sharp, and members of my consultation group, who challenge me to continue honing my therapist skills; and my clients, who continue to grant me the privilege of witnessing their emotional growth.

I acknowledge the American Psychological Association; eTS Marketing; John Wiley & Sons, Inc.; Landmark Editions; Learning Multi-Systems; Live Wire Media; *Maclean's*; Lynne Namka, Ed.D.; the National Film Board of Canada; New Harbinger Publications; the Substance Abuse and Mental Health Services Administration's National Mental Health Information Center; Weekly Reader Publishing and David Wexler, Ph.D. for their generous sharing of resources.

Those who have directly played a more personal part in this publication are my copy editor, typographer and book designer, Susan Ferguson, for her encouragement and efficiency; my cover designer and illustrator, Valerie Knight, for her enthusiasm and creativity; Marty Gilliland at United Graphics Incorporated for his kind help with the printing process; and my colleagues and building mates Carolyn Bray, Lief Corroon,

Susan Glick, Nick Parsons and Michael Quirke, whose interest in the progress of my project motivated me to bring it to completion.

Finally, I acknowledge the steadfast help and support of my husband, Jimmy. He cheered me on during all the ups and downs of writing, editing and re-editing throughout the past three years and always displayed confidence that this book would be published.

I feel blessed to have had the assistance of all these people in so many different ways. Thanks to you all.

Mary Ellen Halloran

Disclaimer

The information contained in this book is not intended to be used to diagnose or treat a mental or physical health condition. If you are concerned about your anger or that of another, please consult a competent professional.

I dedicate this book to my father.

Introduction

I have chosen the title of this book for its symbolism. The tiger is one of the zodiac signs in Chinese astrology. In Chinese Buddhism it personifies Anger. One legend tells of a little schoolboy who had been harshly whipped by his tutor until "stripes" showed on his skin. Furious at his tutor, he ran into the woods. It was there that the boy changed into the first tiger. An untamed tiger, therefore, is considered to be a ferocious and angry creature. If you've ever visited the tiger cage at a zoo or watched a circus act, you may have seen a tiger show his sharp, white teeth as he growled. When we experience our own untamed anger and rage, we get out of control, raise our voices and yell. It's as though sharp, white teeth of our own suddenly become exposed, much like the tiger's. If we don't accept our responsibility as stewards of the tiger, and its counterparts, it will become endangered. If we don't learn how to manage our anger, we will endanger ourselves.

Anger is an intrinsic part of the range of human emotion. We connect with this part when we allow ourselves to feel angry energy within us. However, many of us have been trained to dislike, and even disown, our feelings of anger. Ignoring our anger is risky. If we fail to acknowledge these feelings, we become self-critical when our anger does get aroused. On the other hand, if we accept our anger as a valid emotion, and acknowledge that it is part of the wide range of emotion that is inherent in each one of us by virtue of being human, we enable ourselves to tap into a source of power that lies within each of us. When we recognize <u>all</u> the parts of ourselves, even the parts we sometimes wish we did not have, we are better able to sustain our relationships with ourselves and with others, because we enter relationships as whole persons. Wholeness provides strength. If we are strong, we can be powerful.

In my work as a marriage and family therapist, I have become aware of the pervasiveness of suppressed or explosive anger and the damaging effects anger can have when it is not expressed and managed appropriately. My intention in writing this book is to provide a framework for understanding anger and to facilitate a discussion of how we experience it throughout childhood, adolescence and adulthood and within the context of typical everyday relationships with our partners, children, co-workers and other people we encounter in our daily lives. I address interpersonal dynamics and circumstances that provoke anger, and I offer a healthy way of viewing anger as well as guidance for experiencing and expressing it.

As you read, I invite you to try to recognize the ways in which your own childhood experience has affected your relationship with anger. The purpose of this view into your past is not to blame your past caregivers but rather to understand where you are coming from and to decide where you are headed and where you wish to go in terms of relating to anger.

There are no "cookie-cutter" instructions in the pages that follow, although there are techniques and strategies for you to try. If you have chosen to read this book, it may be that you have tended either (1) to flee from your anger, hiding it or avoiding it at all costs for fear that it would damage your significant relationships, or (2) to fight, expressing your anger hurtfully. I encourage you to search not for ways to avoid your anger but for ways to embrace it and use it in a healthy manner. My hope is that through your reading you can begin to give yourself permission to feel your anger and to find effective, respectful ways of expressing it that match your own particular temperament.

Part One

Understanding Anger

1

Anger Here, Anger There, Anger Everywhere

Anger is real and it is everywhere. It is a natural, healthy human response to circumstances that trigger disappointment, hurt, sorrow or other uncomfortable feelings. Although it can be a manifestation of strength, for a lot of people it is a very difficult and perplexing emotion. There is evidence that it has been part of the human experience since time was first recorded. Anger has a purpose. It's our reaction when something is not right — an indicator that it's time to do what we can to bring about some needed change. When we see that it has a purpose, we can better understand that we are in fact "hard-wired" to feel anger. We can acknowledge it, do something about it if we choose, and then release it. I'll say more about this later.

First, let's look at ways in which anger is symbolized around us. I've chosen some of my favorite examples from nature, history, art, literature and religious works.

Nature

Nature itself produces physical symbols of "anger," albeit violent at times. When volcanoes erupt and earthquakes tremble, they release pressure that has been building deep within the earth. I think of these as signs of the "earth's anger." The movement that must occur deep within the earth is a symbol for the anger in our own personal lives that signals us that something needs to shift or change.

When I use potentially destructive volcanoes and earthquakes as symbols for anger, I do not mean to condone human venting or violence in any form. My intention is to help you to recognize anger as natural — but keep in mind that for humans to act out their anger in violent or hurtful ways is *not* natural, because that type of acting out disregards other natural human characteristics such as compassion and empathy. Although we humans understand that anger is a natural emotion, we also have the intelligence to strive to become more skilled at behaving reasonably when we do get angry. Knowledge of how anger operates within us can enable us to find strength in expressing our anger while maintaining care and empathy for the people around us.

History

History presents us with numerous examples of anger. There has been righteous anger over genuine injustices, leading to landmark events such as the Revolutionary and Civil wars in the United States and the crusade for women to win the right to vote. Significant change has taken place throughout centuries because historical heroes chose to express their anger. The end products of anger have not always been favorable, however. The past is also full of examples of unscrupulous acts of violence that were driven by blind hatred: the activities of the Ku Klux Klan, the Holocaust, and acts of terrorism throughout the world. The perpetrators of these acts allowed their anger to drive them to inhumanity. These inhumane acts are examples of improper and extreme acting out of anger.

Art

It's been said that art imitates life. This appears to be true, because the theme of anger is present in many classic masterpieces. In the sixteenth century, Italian Court painter Dosso Dorsi painted a series of works depicting aspects of the human character, including one on anger. In the seventeenth century, Sir Peter Paul Rubens designed a tapestry entitled *The Anger of Achilles Against Agamemnon*, depicting a section of Homer's

Iliad. More recently, twentieth-century painter Patrice Brisbois has created a series of works entitled *The Seven Deadly Sins,* including one that she calls *Colère (Anger).* Finally, based on a newspaper photograph taken after the disasters of September 11, 2001, Arthur Cadieux painted a large powerful work which he named *Anger.*

Literature

Classical literature throughout the centuries deals with the topic of anger as well, from *Beowulf* in the twelfth century to Shakespeare in sixteenth-century England to Molière and Racine in seventeenth-century France to the eighteenth-century Grimm Brothers in Germany to nineteenth-century Tolstoy in the Russian novel *Anna Karenina.* It goes without saying that current literature across the globe contains treatment of the issue.

Religious Works

It may come as a surprise to some that religious works also contain many references to anger. In the Book of Exodus in the Old Testament of the Bible, Moses becomes angry at the Israelites for dancing around the golden calf. Christians are familiar with the story of Jesus who, upon entering the Temple of Jerusalem and finding that it had been turned into a market-place by moneychangers and others who sold sacrificial ani-mals, wielded a whip and burst out in anger.

Both the Bible and the Koran, the Islamic Book of Faith, have passages that refer to the "wrath of God." Regrettably, this instills a sense of dread into our relationship with God, much like the fear a child has of an angry parent. It is curious to me that, despite this, anger tends to be viewed among reli-gious groups as a barrier to spirituality. It and other negative emotions are often considered evil, feelings to be eliminated if one is to achieve spiritual reward. I can recall my own religion teachers advocating the practice of restraint and self-discipline over the expression of anger, which was labeled "sinful." If we were angry, we personified Satan. There seemed always to be a denial that anger could ever be appropriately expressed. I believe this denial created a split between spirituality and anger, making them mutually exclusive and generating feelings of guilt and shame within us when we did feel angry. As I recall, the same teachers often espoused the Golden Rule[1] — paraphrased as "treat others as you would have them treat you." There was a catch here. Of course, no one relished the idea of being the target of anyone's anger. This left us the option of suppressing our anger so that no one ever had to hear it and deal with it, or if we did express anger, of feeling disappointed in ourselves for failing to follow the Golden Rule as it was being interpreted. What a dilemma: Expressing anger was viewed as bad, yet suppressing it didn't feel so good, either.

Even certain Eastern religions view anger as something to be transformed as quickly as possible into forgiveness. Buddhists strive to transform anger into a positive emotion such as compassion, because anger is considered to be always destructive as well as a sign of weakness, whereas compassion is considered to be a "higher truth." It is difficult to replace anger with a positive emotion if in fact one is sincerely feeling angry, particularly in those cases where the anger is just. The question this raises is, how are we supposed to deal with anger-provoking situations and remain true to our inner experience if we cannot express anger? Compassion and forgiveness are noble goals, but they seem to come much later on in the process.

The risks associated with unexpressed anger are great. Research psychologists who have spent decades studying violent and aggressive behavior have found that aggressive individuals are those who actually have strong reservations about displaying any form of violence and who hardly ever show anger, regardless of how forcefully they are provoked. They fear that if they express their anger they may say something that they don't mean and that they wouldn't otherwise say, or that they may be hurtful for the sake of being hurtful. When, one day, they can't take it anymore, the violence and aggression comes out in devastating ways. Problems like these develop when people are afraid to talk about their anger. I will discuss specific examples of this phenomenon later.

So, the issue is one of containing anger versus discharging it. I believe that understanding the role that anger has played in our world — throughout history, in the arts, in religious tradition and in our own everyday lives — helps us to adopt a healthy perspective of its purpose and use. It is possible to feel our anger and not to act it out but rather to let our anger — our tiger — out in a safe and respectful way — on its leash.

ANGER POINTS

- **A**nger is a natural, healthy human emotion.

- **N**ature, history, art, classical literature and religious works contain expressions of anger.

- **G**reat risks are associated with unexpressed anger.

- **E**xpressing anger in a constructive way is beneficial.

- **R**esearch has shown that aggression results from suppressed anger.

2

What Anger Isn't — And What It Is

Anger is a strong emotion, but it also has gradations. If we imagine a measuring stick, we can place the varying degrees of anger in order of intensity, from slight annoyance on one end to extreme rage on the other. Occasionally, each of us feels angry. However, many of us are uneasy about our experience of anger and may even feel ashamed of it at times. We may believe that we should feel happy all the time, and that it is wrong or bad to feel angry or to be in a bad mood. The thought of conflict makes some of us anxious and sick. After all, if we express our anger, we risk receiving a negative response from the people around us. So we become passive.

Clients come to therapy feeling unhappy and dissatisfied after spending years pleasing their partners and children. They have a lot of anger, and they often tell me that they "hate everybody." As they get in touch with the suppressed anger that has built up, they begin to allow themselves to express it. Their families fail to support them in their anger and quickly let them know that they do not like the "new" Mom/Dad/Partner who expresses anger more appropriately than they expressed it in the past. After seeing the reactions of their family members, clients often report that trying to express their anger "gets them in trouble." This causes them to question whether it is worth it for them to express their negative feelings. They struggle with the pull to return to their more familiar (and more appreciated) state of passivity. When they decide to continue to practice

7

assertiveness they choose to exert a dynamic on their relationships that can require other family members to make some adjustments.

We could go through life constantly seeking the approval of others and in the process betray our own feelings by suppressing emotions and behaviors that we think others won't like. However, when we learn how to express our feelings — specifically our anger — in a productive way, we have learned, and are teaching others, that disagreement is inevitable between people who are close and that people *can* talk about their anger respectfully and productively. When we finally allow ourselves to feel our anger and to express it, the people around us feel more connected to us.

Before I begin my exploration of what anger is, let's take a look at what anger is *not*. I like to draw a distinction between anger and rage. Anger that is hurtful is no longer simply anger. It has crossed the line into unrestrained anger, or rage. Unrestrained anger is explosive and vicious. It involves name-calling, blaming, criticizing, insulting and any other form of verbal or physical abuse you can think of. There is an element of anger in rage, but rage goes beyond anger and can escalate to aggressive and violent behaviors.

Rage

Rage can create problems in the workplace and in personal relationships and can affect the overall quality of a person's life. People lose jobs for displaying rage.

We see evidence in everyday life of the damage that results from rage: A disgruntled employee fires a gun at his co-workers in the workplace, one partner in a relationship wounds the other partner during an argument about family finances, a student takes a weapon to school and injures the student who has been bullying him. In each instance, at least one person's inability to express anger effectively results in unrestrained behavior that can bring about tragic consequences.

Unless we understand the distinction between anger and

rage, we may view any form of anger as threatening and uncontrollable and therefore have doubts about our ability to manage it. Anger then gets a bad reputation. If you associate anger with rage, my suggestion that you allow yourself to experience and express your anger may seem very risky. Actually, the anger that I'm speaking of may be unpleasant, but it is not hurtful. It is respectful and not violent.

One of my colleagues advertises his anger management group by distributing a red flier with the picture of a mad bulldog at the top. Uncontrolled anger, or rage, can be like that mad bulldog on the color red. At times it may seem to get you what you want, but it's usually a Pyrrhic victory.[2]

Ultimately the person expressing rage pays a costly penalty. Managed anger feels different. When anger is allowed and expressed appropriately, the experience can be relieving and calming rather than sending the person out of control.

So, what is anger? We can easily find definitions of the word in dictionaries and explanations of it in encyclopedias. There are so many nuances to anger that my thesaurus provides sixty-four synonyms for the word!

But what does anger mean on a more fundamental, everyday level? Anger is our emotional reaction to our sense that we have been wronged. For the student who learns that the paper he turned in late will only receive half the points it would have otherwise received, anger may include feelings of resentment, disappointment and frustration. To the worker who is fired from her job for failing to meet sales quotas, anger may include feelings of outrage, distress, animosity and fear. Anger can evoke many feelings. Feelings are subjective and cannot be identified as rational or irrational. We can, however, view the *concept* of anger objectively and see that it makes sense.

We seem to be programmed when we are young children to expect absolute thoughtfulness, fairness and empathy from others. But absolutes are fantasies. It is inevitable that from time to time we will be frustrated in our desire to get what we want, and this will lead to anger. At one time or another, each of us feels offended or deceived. These actions provoke anger. When we make sense of anger and find approaches for handling it productively, our life takes on a quality of openness. We draw on power that can strengthen our relationships or stir us to do something about wrongs.

Some believe that anger serves no purpose. It is important to realize, though, that our angry reactions are instinctual. According to Sigmund Freud, the father of psychoanalysis, the mind comprises three structures: the id, the ego and the superego. The id represents our instinct or the desires that drive us. We then develop our ego as a way of gratifying our id while also recognizing the reality that the outside world imposes certain limits — that is, the ego recognizes that we can't always get what we want. The superego is our conscience. So, our id includes all our instinctual energy, part of which is anger. We don't *plan* to be angry. Our sense of self is injured when we are hurt or disappointed, and our anger arises in defense of the self that is injured.

It really doesn't matter whether we're angry over an isolated event or over a series of hurts. The challenge is to discover a way to express how we feel in order to bring about necessary changes in our relationships or our environment. If we suppress our anger and allow it to fester, it can eventually erode our self-esteem and turn into hostility toward others. It's a question of whether we can use our anger to help ourselves or whether we will allow it to get in the way.

Having said all of that, I must acknowledge that anger is an emotion that is frequently misconstrued. On the one hand, it can be alarming. It can cause bodily harm, provoke discrimination or hateful rumors, lead to rebellious activities or compulsive behavior, and result in alienation and mental illness. These negative aspects can destroy lives — damaging relationships, hurting others, interrupting employment, creating confusion, having an adverse effect on a person's physical well being, and wrecking hopes for the future. On the other hand, there is a constructive side to anger. It can reveal problems that need to be addressed. When we allow ourselves to feel it, we can explore how we might use it to effect some necessary change.

ANGER POINTS

• All anger is not the same; there are gradations of anger.

• New ways of expressing anger can evoke reactions from family members who are used to your passivity.

• Going beyond anger into rage leads to aggression and violence.

• Emotional reactions to our sense that we have been wronged are understandable.

• Results of out-of-control anger are destructive.

3

Little Children vs. Big Anger

We tend to use euphemisms to refer to anger and to describe someone who is angry. These euphemisms demonstrate the extent to which we avoid the use of the actual word *angry* in our everyday life. We might refer to ourselves as being peeved... upset... ticked off... frustrated... disgusted... bothered... annoyed. Somehow, these words and others like them seem more acceptable than owning up to feeling "angry." It is no wonder then that children learn at an early age to feel uncomfortable or even fearful when they encounter anger. Not only do families fail to teach the word, they also fail to teach children how to talk about anger and how to deal with it.

There may be a connection between our reluctance to use the word *angry* and the ways in which our families managed anger during our childhoods. Rarely do I encounter clients who describe families that embraced the feeling of anger in a healthy manner. Some recall feeling puzzled over the unpredictable anger of other family members who unexpectedly reacted angrily over seemingly minor situations. In some families people frequently snap at each other with impatience. In other families, anger is pent up, leaving each person to simmer and act moody, dwelling privately on bad feelings and resentment. They may eventually explode by shouting or hitting; other times, they continue to deny the anger. Families who deny anger believe that they "shouldn't" feel angry. They try to sweep it under the rug. The problem with this approach is twofold: First, it bothers others because they don't know whether the person is angry at them or at someone else, and secondly, it will undoubtedly foment into bitterness and ill will. However a family chooses to deal with anger will have a significant impact on the children. How the children are taught to react to anger and experience it early in their development will affect how they will react to anger and experience it later on as adults.

Controllers and Pleasers

Another interesting way to view how anger is managed in families is to look at the roles played by the people in the family. Who are the "Controllers," and who are the "Pleasers"? Although they seem to be at opposite ends of the spectrum, Controllers and Pleasers may share one thing in common: each role is an attempt to cope with anger in the family. They merely have different ways of approaching it.

Controllers seek a sense of power, to avoid being wounded by the angry family as a collective or by individual family members whom they perceive to have more power (perhaps the parents or older siblings). They are usually quite direct and outspoken even when they're not sure about their position. As their descriptive name implies, when Controllers become angered by others' behavior, they attempt to control it. Family members see them as manipulators. They feel as though they're always being pushed to do what the Controller wants them to do.

Pleasers, on the other hand, passively take in the family's anger rather than risk the danger of confronting anyone who seems to be more powerful. They appear to be easy going, patient and willing to go along with the group. They also make good listeners, because it is through listening carefully that they perceive what others want in any given situation — and then they adapt themselves accordingly. Pleasers use roundabout ways of dealing with the family's collective anger. They stuff it in an attempt to remain unnoticed and try to talk themselves out of their own anger. If someone asks, they insist that they're not angry. They make excuses for the people who hurt them by saying something like, "She's just having a bad day. She didn't intend to make me feel bad." They are accustomed to blaming themselves: "If I hadn't made that mistake, he wouldn't have had to yell at me." They attempt to rationalize their anger, telling themselves they shouldn't be angry: "It's not such a big deal." As a result, Pleasers over time become withdrawn, miserable and feel powerless. They become numb because they do not allow themselves to feel their anger.

A family's uneasiness with anger may create controlling or pleasing behavior in children. Let's take a look at how this development occurs. Infants first communicate anger by crying when they are three or four months old. They cry when they are not getting something that they want or need. The caregiver tries to quiet the child, sometimes with frustration. Even at the age of three or four months, a child can sense this frustration. When his anger is consistently met in a negative way, he gets the message that anger and assertion are bad. Not only do these children learn at an early age to beware of expressing their own negative emotions, they also learn to feel uncomfortable and possibly unsafe any time anyone around them is angry or disagrees with them. These children may grow into adults who dread having disagreements with anyone. They are likely to turn into Pleasers.

Similarly, parents who believe that it is best to avoid conflict and who have a difficult time tolerating their child's anger tend to either distance themselves from the child or to quiet her by giving in to any and all demands. The child whose parents distance themselves perceives that distancing as rejection. Rejection, when combined with the feeling of anger, creates in the child an additional feeling of powerlessness.

The worst things a parent can do when a child cries are to overreact to the child's feelings or to minimize them. If a parent overreacts, the child may stop crying to placate the parent while still feeling angry, hurt, disappointed or whatever feeling made her cry. If the parent responds more calmly as the child stops crying, the child learns that she's not allowed to express her feelings and that it's better to placate — that is, to be a Pleaser. Although the crying has stopped, the child may continue to feel angry but now doesn't have a means of expressing it. As a result, she begins to associate anger with powerlessness. This association affects the child's ability to develop a healthy relationship with her anger.

On the other hand, if a parent himself is a Pleaser and appeases his child by satisfying every demand in order to maintain peace, the child learns to use expressions of anger as a manipulative tool to obtain the desired effect. When this happens time after time, the child assumes the role of a Controller. In a sense, the parent allows himself to be trained into compliance by the child. In an interesting turn of events, Pleasers risk producing Controllers and Controllers risk producing Pleasers!

Toddlers

An infant growing into the toddler years enters a period that is naturally fraught with struggles. It is typical for bursts of anger to occur among children who are one to two years old as they learn to exist independently of their parents. As the toddler grows more conscious of his mother as an individual person, he also develops the capacity to experience jealous feelings. He may frequently grow angry at other kids or grown-ups who appear to be taking away even a little of his mother's affection and interest. The toddler also butts up against limitations set by the parents and feels frustrated over not being able to control his environment. He becomes angry, for example, when his movements are confined. The classical power struggle ensues.

If a child is not allowed to experience frustration because his parents give in too easily or because he is consistently told to be quiet and suppress his anger, the child's development in terms of tolerating that anger and the anger of others will be stunted, and the potential for future controlling or pleasing behavior exists. It may also affect the future physical safety of the child as he grows older. Psychologists have noted that accident-prone people are those who suppress their anger and do not communicate their feelings in words.

A child's anger is not easy to tolerate if adults do not understand the reason for the anger. Suppose, for example, that a mother works outside of the home. Her child, who may be too young to understand the reason for Mom's absence every day, misses her. Regardless of who takes care of the child when the mother can't be there and how much fun the child may have during the day, the child misses Mom *and* feels angry at her. The mother may not understand that her child can miss her and feel angry with her at the same time. At the end of the day when they are reunited, the first thing the child does is to throw a tantrum. If Mom scolds her child for this display of anger, the child internalizes the message that she is bad and may begin to conclude that she herself is responsible for her Mom's departure each day because she is so unlovable that Mom does not want to be around her. If Mom understands that the tantrum reflects her child's anger at being separated from her all day, Mom may be able to acknowledge the anger and respond to the source of it in a more nurturing way. This would provide the child with the affectionate attachment she has been wanting all day.

Middle Childhood

Children in middle childhood (ages six to twelve) normally become angry because of restrictive rules or ultimatums, because they feel ignored, or because they're disappointed over not achieving a desired goal. But they find it hard to think about being angry with people they love. Consequently, when a child is not given permission to express anger, she may hide it in order to retain the affection of Mom or Dad. In doing so, the child is hiding an important element of herself. Despite efforts by parents and caretakers to squelch a child's expressions of anger, she will naturally feel angry when something seems unfair. When she wants something she can't get, she will probably cry and even slap siblings to express her disappointment and anger. The significant adults in her life may dislike the child's behavior, but if they do not accept her anger, the child thinks that she can't be angry because it wouldn't be pleasing to Mom or Dad. Children who are angry but quiet usually eventually explode in anger. The explosion at last communicates the built-up anger. When the explosion occurs, the pent-up feelings of anger can be seen in acting-out behaviors. I have worked with children who have demonstrated their anger by suddenly dumping figures into the sand tray in a huge pile. Their anger feels overwhelming to them. They choose to show me how it feels by overwhelming the tray.

Sibling Rivalry

Sibling rivalry is actually a way for children to learn tolerance for their own anger and the anger of their peers. Through fighting with their brothers and sisters and making up afterward, children find out that the display of anger does not mean the end of a relationship. The child learns that after they get angry they can also make up. When children do not get along with siblings and feel jealous toward them, parents often intervene and punish the angry child. This causes the child to judge himself as "not nice." Not only does it affect the child's self-esteem but he doesn't learn how to process his feelings of jealousy and anger. Sometimes a child will find a way to act out these feelings by presenting what appears to be a medical or emotional problem. For example, suppose a four-year-old who has been successfully toilet-trained feels jealous of his new baby sister. If his parents tell him that he is selfish to feel jealous and that he is lucky and should feel happy to have a new baby sister, he may regress to wetting the bed at night. In this indirect way, he expresses the anger that he was not allowed to express directly and without guilt.

Children of Divorced Parents

In my practice I sometimes work with children whose parents have divorced or separated. Studies have shown that a disproportionate number of angry children have parents who are divorced. This means that children in intact families tend to be less angry. Parents often do not recognize that the divorce or separation also causes their children to experience confusion and disappointment. Some children even feel responsible for having caused their parents to split up. While the parents themselves are adjusting to living apart, the children often experience fear of what the future will bring and often feel abandoned and rejected by the parent that has moved out. These feelings — confusion, disappointment, guilt, shame, hurt, abandonment and rejection — are the underpinnings of the child's anger. I once worked with a child who felt rejected by a divorcing parent. In one session, we played a game in which we were to think of feelings we had felt recently, write the feeling word on a piece of newspaper, crumple it up, and throw it into a basket. The point of the exercise was to talk about ways to manage our feelings before they overflow out of us, like the balls of crumpled newspaper could overflow out of the basket. This child wrote the words *hurt, mad* and *angry* over and over on pieces of newspaper, until the basket overflowed. He was telling me very clearly which feelings were overwhelming him. No wonder he was acting out at home and in school. His parents were so involved in their own feelings about the divorce that they had not thought to pay attention to how it was affecting him. Children adjust best following divorce when they have opportunities to talk about their anger and underlying feelings with both parents.

The next time you're around an angry child who hasn't been taught to use her words to express her anger, notice what the child looks like and how she acts out her anger. She may pout. She may harass friends in the schoolyard. She may grit her teeth or make fists as if to strike someone. In fact, she may actually hit, especially if she is around other kids who hit or *if the adults in her life hit her or each other.* Decades ago, nearly all parents hit their children. If you hit your children, your parents probably hit you, and it would not shock me to hear that your grandparents hit your parents. However, researchers who have studied the correlation between frequent spanking at a young age and behavior problems have concluded that some children who are spanked regularly are at greater risk of having behavior problems than kids who aren't spanked. These behavior problems are within a range significant enough for the child's teacher to ask to meet with the parents. In some cases the problems are determined to be severe. The reason is that kids who are spanked are being taught that it is okay to act aggressively. Their acting-out behavior is reflective of the model they are learning from their parents. When the spanking is accompanied by yelling and verbal abuse, the experience is all the more traumatizing for a child.

So, children are *born with* the ability to feel anger, but they are *taught* how to relate to the anger in themselves and others. If the adults in their lives do not teach productive ways of dealing with conflict, children will use non-productive ways. If a child is not encouraged to express his anger appropriately, he may act it out in destructive ways such as stealing, lying or threatening and bullying other children in school. Then, when he receives a negative response and punishment for these behaviors, the child becomes angrier, and a vicious cycle develops. Parents who discipline their children harshly risk losing the child's love. A child who cannot love his parents begins to hate himself as well. Sometimes the result is devastating, not only to the child and the family but also to society in general, as we see in the tragic true story that follows.

The Story of Charles Whitman

Charles Whitman was born in 1941 to a wealthy, prominent family. On the surface the family seemed to have everything. No one knew that Charles's dad had a temper and acted his anger out toward his wife and children. The father admitted to beating his wife on numerous occasions but insisted that he loved her and that he beat her because his temper flared when she became stubborn. He imposed rules on his three sons and, when they did not meet his expectations, meted out physical discipline using "weapons" in the form of belts and paddles or his fists. When Charles was almost eighteen, his father beat him and nearly drowned him in the family's pool. Soon after that beating, Charles enlisted in the Marine Corps and became an excellent sharpshooter. Through a military scholarship program, he was given the opportunity to study engineering at the University of Texas in Austin. However, enrollment in the university gave him his first taste of freedom after a childhood of rigid discipline and a break from the regimented life of a Marine. He got arrested, began to gamble, and earned poor grades. As a result, the Marine Corps withdrew his scholarship and ordered him back into active duty. During this time Charles had also married and was beating his wife as he had seen his father beat his mother. He found the structure and discipline of the Marines to be oppressive, and resentment built up, which he acted out by getting into trouble in many ways.

Finally his father pulled strings to reduce Charles's enlistment time and he was honorably discharged in 1964. Charles returned to Austin determined to do better, but he continually berated himself when he failed to succeed. He experienced bouts of anger, which further eroded his self-esteem. Charles's wife became the breadwinner for the two of them, another sign of failure in Charles's eyes. He displayed a calm exterior, but inwardly he hated himself. His parents separated and divorced after yet another incident of domestic violence. After that, Charles sank deeper into depression and his anxiety increased. A psychiatrist who saw him at that time described Charles as an all-American boy who carried a lot of hostility within him. Charles told the psychiatrist that he hated his father. He continued to try hard at his studies, but amphetamine use hindered his efficiency. Again, his self-esteem suffered. On August 1, 1966,

Charles killed his mother and his wife in their homes and twelve other people in a 96-minute shooting spree from the University of Texas Tower before being killed by Austin police officers.

I suppose that, depending on our perspective, we can attribute this terrible outcome to a number of different things: materiality, alcohol and drug abuse, addictive personality and parental divorce. However, I can't help thinking that, if Charles had been raised by parents who modeled how to deal with negative feelings in a healthy way, he might have lived a different kind of life.

Children whose parents spank them regularly learn to lie about their behavior and their feelings because they fear that if they tell the truth they may be punished. Some children choose not to act out but instead "act in" by carrying their anger and other emotions in their bodies. Their bodies then act out through headaches, stomachaches and other physical symptoms.

All of this shows us that children are significantly affected by their own and others' mismanaged anger, whether it is displayed outwardly or pent up inside. Some may feel as though their anger buries them, as though they are at the bottom of the pile of figures in the sand tray, with no room to move and no air to breathe. Others may feel too scared to express it or experience it, except to stuff it inside of themselves. Furthermore, if adults overreact with their own anger or respond to children's anger as though it were abnormal, a child will often show signs of depression. After all, turning the feelings inward in depression may be perceived by the child to be safer than the consequences of showing anger outwardly.

So, it's valuable to a child to have adults in his life who listen to and validate his anger. Anger is the result of an underlying feeling within the child. For example, if he has been emotionally wounded in some way — and parents and friends, by virtue of being human, will emotionally wound children from time to time — then the natural reaction will be hurt and anger. Allowing a child to feel and express his dissatisfaction with Mom, Dad or any other caretaker is a gift to the child. Forcing a child to hide anger is, in a sense, killing a human emotion that is essential to the child's existence. Enabling a child to feel the anger and teaching him how to manage it will keep the child emotionally healthy.

Children and Sports

The current popularity of team sports for both boys and girls raises another issue for parents, teachers and coaches to address. At the risk of being labeled a "bad sport," the child who is performing badly and feels angry with herself internalizes her self-attacks and keeps them a secret. Unless parents and coaches provide her with an opportunity to release these feelings after the game, she will repeatedly replay a mental tape highlighting her own faults. This is severely damaging to a child's self-esteem. A child who is given tools for expressing anger learns to accept all of herself, including mistakes and negative emotions. She is then better prepared to deal with the mistakes and negative emotions of others. This will serve the child well as she grows up. Because she has learned to cope with uncomfortable feelings, she is better equipped to avoid judging herself and others or pretending that nothing is wrong.

Teens

During adolescence (thirteen to nineteen years of age) a child experiences another round of power struggles, this time not only with parents but also with teachers and other authority figures. Again at this age the child cannot always get what he wants, and things are not always the way he would like them to be. It's a confusing stage of development. Sometimes teens are expected to act like adults, and yet, sometimes they're treated like children. Teenagers encounter many emotions as they mature. They become angry when they feel misunderstood or discounted. Their feelings range from annoyance to deep resentment toward anyone or anything that reminds them that they're not always in control of a situation. In fact, they often can't understand what determines when they get to control and when they don't get to control. Consequently, the world seems unfair. This makes them angry. As they did when they were toddlers, they're learning to separate from their parents and to declare healthy independence, but this time the stakes are higher. They're confronted with uncertainty about individuality, relationships and goals — and the last thing they want is input from their parents. Teenagers' anger at the perceived injustices in their lives is frequently directed not only toward their parents but also toward other adults and the human race in general.

Often teens are expected either to hold back their feelings or to deal with them on their own. They seek relief by bonding with their peers, perhaps in gangs. Here they find others who identify with them. However, voicing anger among peers may not solve a problem and may in fact fuel the anger, turning it into rage. If they are not given tools for dealing with their anger, teens may take aim at unlikely targets. News reports contain stories of adolescents who act out destructively toward others. In 1999 two students at Columbine High School in Littleton, Colorado, killed twelve students and one teacher during a shooting rampage that ended when the two students took their own lives. In 2001 a fifteen-year-old student at Santana High School in San Diego County, California, shot and killed two classmates and wounded thirteen other people at the school because he was depressed from the mocking and bullying he was experiencing. These shootings are a tragic example of the acting out of unresolved anger. Because the relationship between teens and their parents shifts as teens grow increasingly more autonomous, parents and family members do not realize how vulnerable their adolescents are to feeling rejected by their immediate or extended family. Teens who act out violently often report having felt like outcasts prior to their acts of violence. Their feelings of rejection turn into rage, and the result is devastating. It can be intolerable for an adolescent to deal with his hurts all by himself, so he turns on other people in anger and sometimes rage. The acting out may numb the hurts, but it does nothing to bring about healing.

So adolescents act out in a variety of ways to relieve their emotional pain, which is most commonly rooted in feelings of sadness, jealousy, inferiority, anxiety, loneliness, hopelessness, boredom, frustration and stress. Acting out can take the form of hostile body language, verbal insults and physical attacks. Often kids who act out in these ways have grown up in wounding environments, without the opportunity to express their anger and have it accepted by adults who care. Risky behaviors can also be connected to the emotional pain that underlies anger.

Running away from home is one example of risky acting-out behavior. Researchers who have studied the relationship between homelessness and family violence (that is, unmanaged anger) have concluded that family violence is a primary factor in teens' decisions to leave home. When their families are angry, the kids are angry, and they act out their anger by risking their own safety.

In addition to running away from home, some teens become addicted to drugs and alcohol in an attempt to change their painful reality. Some engage in prostitution, and some even commit suicide. Teen suicide often occurs after a teen has experienced rejection. Family members of adolescents who commit suicide look back and recall that the teen's character changed shortly before the suicide. Often they recall that she displayed uncharacteristic anger. It seems likely that the anger was due to the feelings of rejection. Suicide has been described as an expression of rage. As noted earlier, anger is a signal that something needs to change. Unfortunately, suicide changes the picture in a final, devastating way.

ANGER POINTS

• Anger is uncomfortable for many families.

• Neither Pleasers nor Controllers manage family anger in a healthy way.

• Growing up without permission to express anger affects a child's future ability to deal with anger.

• Expressions of anger — verbal and physical — are passed down from one generation to the next.

• Risky behaviors can be associated with the emotional pain that underlies a teen's anger.

4

The Very Angry Girl Becomes a Very Angry Woman

Another perspective of anger that warrants our attention here is the societal expectations of girls and boys with respect to anger. In more than one study researchers found that when strangers believe that a crying baby is a male, they most likely take it for granted that the baby is crying from anger. When they believe that the crying baby is a female, they believe the baby is afraid. Girls are just not expected to be angry.

"Nice girls don't get mad."

Expressing anger in our society can be difficult for girls, who often receive the message as they grow up that they should be "ladylike." A familiar nursery rhyme asserts that girls are made of "sugar and spice and everything nice." About the same age that girls are learning this rhyme, they are also receiving other messages that convey to them that being angry is "not nice." This does not eliminate their feelings of anger but it makes girls unwilling to talk about these feelings. In fact, they begin to believe that they *shouldn't* feel angry. They grow into adulthood feeling uncomfortable about their anger. Therefore, they try to deny it altogether. If anger is suppressed often enough and long enough, it is possible for a girl eventually to have trouble even knowing that she is angry.

Because girls are often trained in childhood to suppress their anger and to view it as something unbecoming to them, many women are afraid to say, "I feel angry." The ability to express their anger has been socialized out of them. Instead, they deny their anger by stuffing it or telling themselves that "it doesn't help to be angry." Actually, these responses lead to greater anger because they cause a woman to invalidate her own feelings. It comes as no surprise to me that, when women finally do articulate anger, they may become overwhelmed. Tears often accompany the feeling of being overwhelmed. As we have seen, crying is the way that a child expresses anger. Within every very angry woman is a very angry child waiting for the chance to express her feelings.

You may recall the child in the previous chapter whose mother left home every day to go to work. Let's suppose this child is a girl. She became angry with her mother because she *missed* her mother. If the child's anger is not acknowledged and given space by her mother, the feeling of abandonment that underlies her anger is like a seed that has been planted that can grow into intense anger later in her life. As an adult woman, she may experience reminders of her childhood feeling of abandonment and may blame herself when others choose to leave, seeing it as further evidence that she is too unlovable to be around. This belief can eventually damage her adult relationships. If, in fact, she had been able to express her anger as a child and her mother had accepted it, she would be better equipped to manage her adult anger at feeling abandoned and not internalize others' departures as evidence that something is inherently wrong with her.

Women's Anger Can Bring Change

One of my favorite classical myths describes a mother who was driven by her anger to take drastic measures to achieve the release of her daughter from the Underworld. I think it effectively describes how a woman's anger can be used to bring about desired change. Briefly, this is the story:

Kore, a young girl, was picking flowers in a meadow. As she reached for a blossom, the earth unexpectedly opened wide, making way for a golden chariot to exit from below, drawn by black horses and driven by Hades, Lord of the Underworld. The girl screamed for help but no one was nearby. Hades abducted her and took her to his realm deep inside the earth. When Kore failed to return home, her mother Demeter searched for her for nine days and nights. She dressed in dark clothes, continually calling her daughter's name and refusing to eat, drink or rest. On the tenth day Demeter went to the city of Eleusis in the guise of an old woman. The King and his wife welcomed her into their home. During her stay, the swineherd of the King's family told Demeter of a huge hole in the earth that had swallowed his swine. He told her that a chariot had appeared and dashed down into the chasm. The chariot driver had a shrieking young girl clasped in his arm. Surmising that the kidnapper was her brother Hades, Demeter confronted Helios, the sun, who sees all, and persuaded him to confess that Hades was the villain. Demeter realized that Zeus, king of the gods, who was brother to both Hades and Demeter, had known about Hades but had chosen to ignore Demeter's sorrow and Hades's crime.

Demeter in her anger continued to roam the earth, forbidding the trees to produce fruit and the herbs to grow, until the entire human race was at risk of extermination. Zeus had no choice but to tell Hades to return Kore to her mother. He told Demeter that she could have her daughter back, provided Kore had not consumed any food in the Underworld.

However, because Kore had already eaten seeds of a pomegranate, Hades claimed her as his own. Demeter, increasingly angry, threatened to go on destroying the fruits of the Earth. At last a concession was reached. Kore would spend part of the year with Demeter and the other part with Hades, reigning as Persephone, Queen of the Underworld.

Demeter's anger brought about the return of her daughter, whom she loved very much and who had been taken away from her. Having to be without her daughter was a situation that had to change, as far as Demeter was concerned. When a woman understands that her anger can serve a worthwhile purpose by bringing about desired change, she can free herself from the concept that "nice girls don't get mad," and allow her expression of anger to work for her when appropriate.

Some of my female clients seek therapy to overcome their anger issues. They've usually decided that they're going to start expressing themselves, and they've made some awkward attempts, but they have hurt friends' feelings in the process. They conclude that they have a problem controlling their anger. I suggest to them that they don't need help *controlling* their anger; they need help *acknowledging* it and *expressing* it. After all, anger has always run counter to the expectations of others that they be "nice." I tell these clients that I can help them to let their anger out more effectively, but I will not help them to suppress it once more and pretend it isn't there. That's unhealthy. I help them to begin to feel comfortable stating, "I feel angry because ...." Through practice, women can acquire the skills for letting others know that they're angry and talking about it calmly. They find that they no longer avoid the anger or experience a familiar guilt over having felt it, nor do they express it in ways that damage relationships and make matters worse.

A lot of conflict in families today is due to "recycled anger." If anger remains unacknowledged and unexpressed, it passes from generation to generation — it gets recycled. I was dismayed to discover in my research that some sources claim that the early settlers in America, while declaring wife-beating to be illegal, retained a common-law principle which made it acceptable for a man to strike his wife with a switch no thicker than his thumb.[3] Apparently, a wife had no choice but to tolerate the abuse if her husband exercised his legal right. Whether or not this is factual, we know that spousal abuse exists today and that there are women who suffer abuse in silence.[4]

Women who are beaten by their partners and remain silent about it are often from families that have patterns of violence. I see female clients who eventually talk about the anger they feel on behalf of past generations of women in their families who allowed themselves to be abused by men. Finally, in their own therapy, these clients face the challenge of either repeating that multigenerational pattern or allowing themselves to feel their anger and to find appropriate ways to release it. They begin to come to terms with past emotional injuries, and they choose to give themselves permission to express their anger, at least in therapy, toward the people who have hurt them. I watch them grow from women who were afraid of anger into women who find healing by expressing it.

ANGER POINTS

• **A**n ability to display anger can be an outgrowth of societal expectations.

• **N**iceness is often considered synonymous with absence of anger.

• **G**irls need help acknowledging and expressing their anger as they develop.

• **E**ffective expression of anger eliminates suppression of anger.

• **R**ecycled anger is anger that passes without resolution from generation to generation within a family.

5

The Very Angry Boy Becomes a Very Angry Man

"Boys will be boys!"

Anger seems to be accepted, and sometimes even expected, as part of male behavior. Myths and legends are filled with stories of male figures that are described as "strong" and "brave." It is rare to find a story depicting a male hero who admits to feeling fear or who cries. He is most often aggressive and intimidating. It may even be that anger is the only emotion that some male heroes portray. These stories support the traditional societal expectation that boys avoid showing fear and pain. When they fall and hurt themselves, they're told, "Big boys don't cry." Consequently, in their desire to be thought of as a "big boy," they relinquish their tears. They learn not to show their sadness, grief, hurt or fear. Often they transform these primary feelings into anger, using it as a secondary emotion to enable them to cope. Yet, some male clients have told me that they don't let themselves experience anger because they fear they could become dangerous to themselves and others. I gather from this fear that, like girls, boys also do not receive tools during their developmental years to help them feel their anger and express it, rather than having it take them over.

Boys eventually learn that anger counterbalances the feelings they are hiding, and as they grow older they become adept at using it as a defense. Anger then becomes linked to masculinity and power. However, using expressions of anger as a defense is misdirected. Rather than expressing anger honestly and respectfully, many men use it as an attempt to control another person's behavior in order to make their own fear, pain or worry go away.

Although there are many young women in the military, I view war as an extreme example of collective male anger that can be acted out in a misguided way. Countries wage war because their leaders are angry, and they use their anger as a justification for fighting. A nation's media presents photographs and film of the military equipped with powerful weapons intended to destroy the opponents. The images in fact are symbolic of the desire to control the enemy in order to eliminate the fear, pain and worry created by the enemy's existence.

Aggression in Contact Sports

Boxing, football, rugby, soccer and wrestling — all predominantly male sports — are excellent forms of exercise and healthy catharses of energy. Athletes who participate in these sports tend to be bigger because they must withstand the force of physical contact. But because of the size and strength of the players, the competitive need to dominate and win can get out of hand and drive athletes to aggression, posing risks for participants.

In a recent World Cup soccer game, a player head-butted an opponent in the chest with such force that it could have resulted in serious injury or death to the opponent. Even the spectators of these sports take on an aggressive demeanor, as evidenced by stampedes at soccer stadiums and various types of out-of-control behavior at other sports events. I attended a National Football League game several years ago. The fans in attendance were equally as aggressive as the players they had come to watch. A mother whose small son was wearing the visiting team's colors feared for his safety after home-team spectators jeered at him on their way into the stadium. I myself felt fearful of the aggressive atmosphere as the loud, massive crowd of ticket holders inched their way through the underground tunnel to their seats.

It's not clear to me whether aggressive men are drawn to contact sports or whether contact sports fuel men's aggression. What is clear is that this aggression has become identified with being male. For this reason, many men develop the false idea that aggression is just a normal part of life. There are frequent media reports of assaults by professional and college athletes on people they encounter off the playing field. Their on-field aggression primes them for inappropriate behavior when they are provoked in some way in their everyday lives. They do not handle their anger well. Neither do their loyal fans.

Similarly, when a man does not "follow the rules" when expressing his anger, his worst fear can become his reality. If he is larger and stronger than the person with whom he is angry and he cannot manage his anger, he does indeed have the potential of becoming volatile and dangerous and causing physical harm.

Nice Guys Can Be Angry Guys

When anger is not managed appropriately by men, it often results in violence. Researchers have found that men experience stress when they feel physically or intellectually inferior. This stress leads to anger, hostility and rage in many men. In addition, men who experience this type of stress often manage their insecurities with substance abuse which in itself makes a guy prone to verbally abusing his partner. The partners of these men can live in constant fear in their own homes, never knowing when the stress is going to escalate. Some men recognize this and attempt to hide their anger. They put a lot of effort into being "nice guys." They may compensate for their discomfort with their anger by attempting to please and saying "yes" more often than they'd like. They get people to like them not because of who they are as a person but because they do not challenge others by standing up for themselves or expressing anger. Actually they are suppressing not only their anger but feelings underneath the anger. Often those feelings include fear — fear of what will happen if they do express themselves. Perhaps their anger will be too ugly. Perhaps it will be overwhelming. Those who know them assume that everything's fine because the guy isn't expressing anger or any other feelings. Then we hear of close family members and friends of men who commit murder and other heinous crimes who are stunned to learn that deep anger and hostility had been buried inside these men for years. Eventually anger finds its way out, and too often it is in a violent way. What materializes is the very thing these men had feared.

David Wexler, Ph.D., who is the founder and executive director of the Relationship Training Institute in San Diego, has done a lot of work in the field of domestic violence. His most recent book is entitled *When Good Men Behave Badly.*[5] I think that the title was well chosen. Good men who do not have the tools to manage their anger do behave badly, potentially resulting in violent situations.

Men who seek my help in managing their anger are initially surprised when I ask them to study a chart of "feeling words" and recall situations in their lives when they have felt anxious, inferior, tired, criticized, embarrassed, hopeless, lonely, sad, stressed and so on. Some have seldom used those words to identify how they felt. Instead, they recall that, in situations that caused them to feel any of these emotions, they very quickly became angry. In fact, they recall that as boys they never heard their fathers or any other older male relatives identify these feelings. What many of them do recall is that their fathers frequently displayed anger but said very little about any other feelings.

David Wexler[6] talks about "masculinity traps." He explains that these are messages that a boy receives as he grows up that are based on the behaviors of significant male figures in his life. They are "traps" because they lure a boy into believing them. In actuality, they provide a distorted view of masculinity that is destructive to relationships. One of these traps is the belief that a man should never show his feelings and should always be tough because, if he shows feelings (other than anger), he appears weak and even effeminate. Just as with any trap, disentangling from these damaging beliefs requires time and effective tools. As long as a man remains stuck within the clutch of a trap, he will suffer from lack of circulation of the wide range of emotions that could be available to him.

ANGER POINTS

- Accepted as part of male behavior, anger is sometimes the only emotion that boys are allowed to display.

- Nice guys may not ever allow themselves to express anger.

- Good men can engage in bad behavior if they have never acquired tools to manage their anger.

- Emotions that underlie anger go unidentified when a man quickly resorts to angry outbursts.

- Relationships are adversely affected when men believe it's unmanly to express their feelings.

6

The Very Angry Woman and Very Angry Man Enter a Relationship

Relationships are complex. Men and women get angry over things their partners say and do. Their anger, however, can actually be a sign of closeness. Clients tell me that they hardly ever get angry with people other than their partners. Your partner is the person you probably most care about and the person who probably has the greatest effect on your life. It's ironic: The person who is capable of providing you with the greatest pleasures is at the same time capable of frustrating and hurting you most deeply. In fact, there's probably no one who can anger you more than your partner.

When you have not been sufficiently trained in earlier years to experience and express your anger, you enter into relationships unable to recognize the preliminary signs of anger build-up in yourself and in your partner — the bodily cues, emotional set-ups and negative self-talk. What do you know, or what have you observed, about your partner's anger? Can you recognize when she is angry? Does she communicate her message straightforwardly and clearly, or is she evasive, or does she clam up? How do you respond to your partner's anger? Often we are not only angry that we ourselves are angry but we become angry that the other person is angry, as well. We are much less susceptible to hurt when we allow the anger and acknowledge the necessity for discharging it productively within our relationship. Many of us become defensive at the first sign of our partner's anger. Are you able to allow her to be angry and to encourage her to express it? Can you accept this anger?

Anger in the Workplace...
Let's take a look at how an angry interaction evolves within a relationship. Suppose you feel angry over something that happened at work. After all, anger is often work-related. Many employees in today's workforce are worried that they will be laid off. Companies are outsourcing or finding ways to get work done with fewer people. There is a great deal of rivalry for a smaller number of jobs. People feel less in control and perhaps even powerless over their own future. Anger over these circumstances, combined with lack of confidence in a person's own abilities, create a stressful work environment.

So, suppose your boss criticizes you, and you feel unjustly reprimanded. When you feel powerless, the only way you can wrest back some semblance of self-esteem may be through the use of anger. Anger is a powerful emotion, and expressing it can make you feel strong. Unfortunately, expressions of anger are not tolerated in many work environments. Employees cannot express their anger in ways that would enable them to work through it and move beyond it. (Workplace anger that cannot be expressed is a serious concern because it can turn into aggression that can lead to tragedy and leave co-workers traumatized. There have been incidents of people who have acted out their anger by returning to their former place of employment to shoot their former boss or co-workers.[7])

...Finds Its Way Home with Us
Anger may make you feel in control of a situation, but suppose you fear that if you express it at your workplace you will lose your job. So, you continue to suppress your anger on the job. This doesn't do anything to lessen it. Because anger is energy, suppressing it is almost certain to intensify it. When workplace anger cannot be resolved effectively, it tends to spill

out into your personal life, most often creating conflicts with your partner. You may have been unable or unwilling to express how you were actually feeling in a given situation at work. Instead, you become angry at the first person you see when you arrive home and walk through the door: your partner. I refer to this displaced anger as anger that "comes out sideways." If you consistently suppress your anger and never deal directly with its source, you will develop the habit of shifting it to another target. When you misdirect your anger and allow it to come out indirectly at your partner, who may be a safer target but in truth is merely an "innocent bystander," your partner thinks it is unfair and becomes hurt and angry in return. Now both of you are angry at the same time. This is fertile ground for a situation to grow out of proportion to the circumstances.

I believe that anger is the most difficult emotion to receive from a loved one. You may not want to listen to your partner's anger because it makes you feel as if you have failed him. It may remind you that your relationship is less than what you'd like it to be. Furthermore, your angry partner is probably not able or willing to provide what *you* need in the moment. Because you're not getting what you need, you're also less able or willing to be empathic with your partner. In fact, you're pretty angry with him. You blurt out angry words, and the words only make the situation worse. What each of you wants most is to be heard and understood. However, in the heat of the moment, neither of you is able to listen to the other because each of you feels hurt. You may have released part of your built-up frustration, but you are still upset over what happened at work because you have not directed your anger at its initial source. Furthermore, your partner is now upset over having been ambushed.

Everyone is entitled to become angry from time to time when situations warrant it. But in your intimate relationship you may not know what to do when your partner gets angry. Because of your own discomfort with the emotion, you may squelch and deny her entitlement to be angry. It is difficult to show empathy to your partner when she exhibits an emotion that makes you uncomfortable. As a result, when she expresses anger, you may reject her.

There's No Magic Cure
There is an old folk story about a husband who has returned back home from combat feeling angry. His wife is so uncomfortable with his anger that she goes on a dangerous mission to obtain a cure for it, only to discover in the end that it cannot be resolved by a magic spell but only through her patience with her husband's mood. When your partner becomes angry, you too may go to any extreme to make the anger go away. But what is your partner supposed to do with his anger if he isn't able to let you know about it? Actually, what your partner needs is your patient reassurance that he is heard and understood.

If the anger were not present and only the feelings underlying the anger were expressed, you might be more likely to empathize with your partner's feelings. After all, it's the underlying feelings that cause your partner to feel weak and vulnerable. These are the feelings that are more likely to evoke your empathy. Think about this for a moment. Would you be more willing to listen to your partner if she stated, "I feel ashamed..." "I feel discouraged..." "I feel inadequate..." "I feel worried..." "I feel overwhelmed..." or "I feel exhausted..." than if your partner were to say, "I feel angry..."? Unfortunately, your potential for being empathic may stay hidden in the face of anger. You do not get to hear the actual feelings underneath your partner's anger if you "punish" your angry partner, as you may have been punished for your own anger in your early years. Depending on your early experience with anger, your partner's anger can cause you to feel as though the world has come to an end. You may have experienced the feeling of severance when anger occurred in early relationships, particularly with your primary caregivers. As small children, feeling cut off from adults who were important to you may have created a fear that you risked losing all your security whenever adults became angry with you. This fear can carry into your adult life, so that when your partner becomes angry you fear losing the relationship. The thought, "She doesn't like me anymore," is a common example of this sort of fear.

One of the reasons why another's anger can be so uncomfortable for you is that when you yourself become angry you are not able to express your anger effectively. You either don't allow yourself, don't have the know-how, or believe it won't be accepted. You begin to believe that anger and other negative feelings should be avoided. In so doing, you invite the very result you are trying to prevent. While you may fear losing the relationship if anger is expressed, actually the opposite is true. The *inability* to express anger leads to relationship problems.

Avoiding anger in relationships is in a sense resigning yourself to having negative relationships, because evading the anger prevents you from seeking positive resolution with your partner. The source of the anger never gets addressed, and it continues to fester and resurface throughout the duration of your relationship.

I've noticed that the inability to express anger in a relationship can create a domino effect. It can lead to fear, envy and sadness. Let's look at how each of these feelings can be an outgrowth of suppressed anger.

Fear

Both men and women can be equally fearful of expressing angry feelings. When you are unable to express your anger at your partner, you may be afraid of what may happen if these feelings somehow get out. You may fear that your partner will criticize or disapprove of your anger. If you don't know *how* to ask for what you want, it can be frightening even to try. You wind up feeling confused, because anger and fear are incompatible. The purpose of fear is to alert you to danger. Fear of anger would send the alert that anger is dangerous. There are two responses to fear: fight or flight. Therefore, if anger is per-ceived as dangerous, you would either fight it (by resisting it) or flee it (by avoiding it).

Anger is a tool that signals that something needs to change. It helps you to rally the strength needed to take action. If you are fighting or fleeing the tool that is supposed to be helping you, you lose the ability to use the tool effectively and derive benefit from its use. Fearing anger, or believing that it has no place in a loving relationship, sabotages a relationship. When couples work hard to maintain "niceness," they never find out how to endure conflict or sustain an angry encounter. Rather than say, "I'm angry," they stop talking and withdraw physical-ly and emotionally from the person they most care about. They don't allow themselves to live spontaneously enough for com-mon angry encounters to occur. Sometimes partners take satis-faction in the fact that they never display angry feelings toward each other. In fact, they don't get to experience trust in the rela-tionship. When trust is in short supply, partners are likely to be more angry and closed off from one another.

Envy

When you feel angry with your partner, there may be something you need or want from him that you're not getting *and* that you feel entitled to. If you are not able to express your anger when you do not get what you feel entitled to, you become displeased with your partner who is not providing it and envious of those who *do* have what you want.

Entitlement causes your anger to boomerang. When you think in terms of what your partner is "supposed to" do for you or give to you, you're viewing her behavior through the narrow lens of your own individual needs and desires rather than view-ing it through a wide lens. The difference is like looking through a funnel toward the narrow end rather than toward the wide end. When you judge your partner's behavior narrowly, you tend to blame her and want to strike back. The anger comes around again — and you're *still* not able to express it.

Focusing only on our own
needs and desires

Focusing on the other person's
needs and desires as well as our own

Illustration 1: Views Through a Funnel

Sadness

Reluctance to express your anger and to ask for the changes you want can lead to two-fold sadness: the sadness of not getting what you want or need and the sadness that you can't advocate for yourself. Each time you fail to express your anger, you become sadder.

There is something you can do to avoid the fear, envy and sadness that are brought on by not expressing your anger. You can learn how to express it. Occasional anger is inevitable in a close relationship, especially if partners are candid about their respective needs. You cannot avoid it. When you meet someone and become romantically involved, you tend to idealize him at first. The idealization cannot last forever. Eventually your partner will need something that will encroach on your own comfort, and you will feel frustrated and inconvenienced. When you are frustrated and inconvenienced, you feel angry. This first feeling of disillusionment, and the subsequent anger, are often thought of as evidence that "the honeymoon is over."

Anger: Let the Tiger Out, But Keep It on a Leash

You need not be concerned if you occasionally get angry with your partner. You should be concerned if you get angry with your partner and consistently fail to express it. Unexpressed anger in a relationship can restrict the potential for creative problem solving. If anger isn't shared openly, problems cannot be resolved successfully. When anger is expressed in a healthy manner, it can motivate you to resolve problems together. Both of you need to develop the capacity to receive and accept anger from each other without punishing each other for it. This requires a commitment on the part of both of you to maintain a relationship that is secure enough to withstand the expression of anger.

If you ever complain of the lack of "spark" in your relationship, the actual problem may not be the lack of romance but your failure to deal with anger in a productive way. When the initial thrill of dating fades, partners who are not able to express their feelings honestly are left to grapple with feelings of monotony and isolation. When your partner teases you, you may feel angry and hurt. If you fail to express your anger and simply "turn off," you are not giving your anger the attention it deserves. It is unresponsiveness to your own anger and that of your partner that can destroy your relationship. Healthy anger helps a relationship to thrive.

If you do not know how to express your anger, when it occurs it triggers fear that the relationship is going to end. But it does not mean that the relationship is threatened or in danger of ending. It is true that when you do not acknowledge and deal with anger in a relationship the risk is that the anger will accelerate and destroy the relationship. Note, however, that it is not the *anger* but its *acceleration* that threatens the relationship. So, anger is destructive to a relationship only if it is not expressed appropriately or if one of the partners has unhealthy reactions to it. Communicating anger in a respectful way strengthens a relationship because it empowers both partners. Making your partner aware that you are angry by expressing it can actually nurture your relationship. Here's an example:

Suppose Taylor feels angry over a perceived lack of support from Kyle during a time of need. If Taylor does not allow herself to express her anger, or if Kyle is not able to hear and accept the anger, Taylor may write Kyle off as thoughtless and uncaring, and their relationship would suffer. But the expression of anger and the acceptance of it can help the relationship to thrive and even improve.

Imagine another scenario: Mel calls Cameron a "lazy jerk" because he did not help with the dishes. Cameron does not feel he merits Mel's insult because he has worked hard all day and is tired, so he reacts in turn toward Mel with angry words and actions. Mel feels that her criticism of Cameron was justified because she, too, had a difficult day. She responds with yet a higher degree of anger. That response causes Cameron to respond with a higher level of anger still. This couple is "stuck in the loop." I draw it as an infinity symbol, because it can go on and on and on:

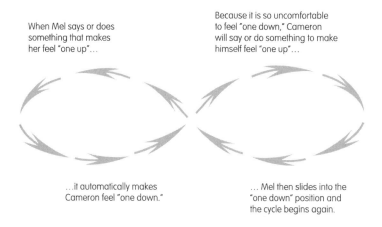

When Mel says or does something that makes her feel "one up"...

Because it is so uncomfortable to feel "one down," Cameron will say or do something to make himself feel "one up"...

...it automatically makes Cameron feel "one down."

... Mel then slides into the "one down" position and the cycle begins again.

Illustration 2: Relationship Loop

This cycle will continue until Mel and Cameron get tired of fighting or someone or something breaks up the fight. But nothing really gets resolved. The next time one of them feels angry, rather than expressing it directly and respectfully, they will find themselves in the loop once again.

When your partner hurts you, you may interpret her actions as deliberate. This will most likely make you angry. Actually, your partner may not have been *trying* to hurt you. In fact, she may not even have knowingly acted in a hurtful way yet you perceived her action to be hurtful. Therefore, you may aim your anger at her because you feel offended. The greater the alleged offense, the more intense your anger will be. Notice in this situation that it is *your judgment* that you have been deliberately hurt that makes you angry. If you are able to express your anger and then listen to your partner's perspective, you can short-circuit the potential damage that your judgment can cause. Communicating up front that you feel angry is the key to avoiding getting into the loop.

A Relationship Is a System

Another way to look at angry behavior styles in relationships is to view a relationship as a system. When one part of the system acts a certain way, the other parts of the system are affected, as well. In a relational system, one person's behavior can provoke a particular behavior on the part of the other person, and so goes the cycle. It's as though one behavior is a set-up for the other. Over time, these set-ups can be hurtful, intensifying negativity between partners. Here's a list of complementary behaviors that can breed hurt, disappointment, resentment and anger if they are used as weapons against each other:
- When A is independent, B is dependent
- When A pursues, B distances
- When A is angry, B withdraws
- When A demands, B resists
- When A attacks, B defends

Self-Talk

Everyone engages in "self-talk." Self-talk is the conversation you have within yourself, the "tapes" that play in your head. When you have suppressed your anger for a long time, your self-talk is angry. Much of your angry self-talk carries over from your childhood. You believe this self-talk, as hurtful as it may be. If your feelings were not respected and you were made to feel unimportant as a child, you may have become determined not to allow anyone to make you feel that way when you grew up. Later, in your adult relationships, when your partner says or does something that makes you feel disrespected or unimportant, you think, "I'm not going to let him treat me like this!" The old feelings that you had as a child get triggered. Old tapes start playing. Consequently, your angry reaction becomes bigger than the incident seems to warrant. The suppressed anger turns into rage (aggression). Raging at someone who has infuriated you may cause you to feel better in the moment, but it also predisposes you to wounding in this way. Being aggressive becomes easier the more you do it. You become desensitized to your own displays of hostility. Research has shown that a person's negative feelings intensify toward another person or group each time he injures them. This cycle is apparent in cases of violence and prejudice. I'll say more about the connection between anger and prejudice later on.

Another example of childhood-related angry self-talk occurs when as a child you were not allowed to express anger with parents or siblings. Although you were forced to suppress your anger, it didn't go away. It stayed inside, building higher and higher as you crossed into adulthood. Let's call this angry part of you the "grown-up child." Enter your partner who says or does something that angers you. The grown-up child within you still does not have the skills necessary to communicate the anger but continues to suppress it as you had always been taught to do. There eventually comes a time when your partner feels hurt by something you have said or done. Your suppressed anger prevents your grown-up child from empathizing, and your partner's grown-up child may get triggered and feel hurt. At this point you are not operating on an adult-to-adult level anymore. If you were, you would both be able to listen to each other and empathize with each other's feelings. At best, you are operating on disparate levels, adult-to-child. This is because the grown-up child within you is still developmentally a child with respect to expressing your feelings. If both of you are "grown-up children," then you will both continue to derive satisfaction at seeing each other hurt, because you consider it "payback time."

Power and Control

When anger in your family was used as a vehicle for power and manipulation, you may have grown up using it to control and manipulate your adult partners. You may try to coerce your partner with angry demands in an effort to be heard and get your way. I have worked with clients who have felt angry with their partners because their partners were unwilling to commit to marriage. Problems arise when these clients cannot express their anger. They feel neglected because they are not getting what they want from their partners. They become needy. The longer their partners remain uncommitted, the more they act out their neediness. They do not have the tools that would allow them to tell their partners how their lack of commitment makes them feel, and they become stuck in their anger. It's another example of inviting just what they want to prevent. Their acting out is self defeating because it results in their partners' questioning even more whether they want to marry them. These clients are like a child who is hurt because he feels neglected, can't ask directly for what he wants, acts out in anger, and gets punished instead of getting the attention he longs for.

Indirect acting out of anger is never effective. It merely serves to alienate and polarize so that you are less likely to hear each other, much less want to satisfy each other. Instead you go on the defensive and push each other away.

This illustration effectively compares the options available to you and the consequences of each:

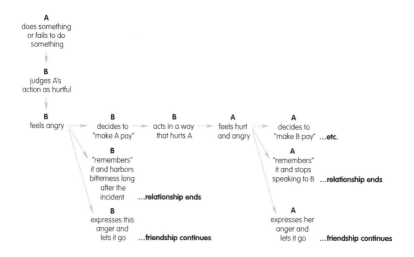

Illustration 3: Options for Coping with Anger

A word about harboring bitterness: continuously rehashing painful memories over a long period of time does damage to your own emotional health as well as to your relationships. When you hold on to injuries without working through them, the significance of the wrong that was done becomes exaggerated as time goes by. You then become angry with everyone you meet. Often after years of severed communication, people will say, "I don't even remember why we stopped talking." In the meantime, the bitterness has prevented them from enjoying people and activities in the present. They dwell upon old events as though they happened yesterday.

If you find that angry feelings are lingering on for a long time, ask yourself, "Do I really want to be this unhappy all the time? How is it serving me to hold onto my anger without doing something about it?" See if you can separate the hurt from the anger. If someone has hurt you, allow yourself to express the hurt and see if it releases the anger. After all, letting go of the anger is in your own best interests. Almost everyone who begins therapy with me is angry with one or more people in their lives. I have come to realize that anger is the source of other emotional problems. It leads to depression, anxiety and all sorts of relationship problems. Chronic feelings of isolation, sadness, worry and overall irritability are common among today's population. These are often symptoms of people who cannot express their angry feelings effectively.

ANGER POINTS

• Anger expressed in a healthy way can actually help a relationship to thrive.

• Not dealing with the true source of your anger can cause anger to "come out sideways" at innocent bystanders.

• Going to great lengths to make your partner's anger go away isn't the answer.

• Empathizing with your partner's feelings can improve a situation.

• Relationships are systems; the behavior of one part of the system affects the other part.

7

A Very Angry Couple Become Parents

W hen a couple is filled with unexpressed anger and resentment, the arrival of children only compounds the troubles in their relationship. Parental anger is most often displayed in two situations: where a parent has inadequately adjusted to the demands of parenting in general and where a parent has difficulties with a particular child's behavior or problems. If parents have not learned how to express their uncomfortable emotions constructively, they will repeat the same patterns they learned as children with their own children. Sometimes kids say and do things that sadden, hurt or confuse their parents. Rather than acknowledging these feelings, parents may withdraw or lash out in anger. It is not possible for you to teach a child to feel anger and express it effectively if you yourself cannot model it through example.

Suppose a mother becomes angry with her infant and strikes her when she cries. Any parent who has ever cared for a baby can attest to the fact that not knowing what to do to stop an infant from crying for hours on end is extremely exasperating. The majority of parents offer compassion and comfort, but the crying can also cause anger and sometimes even abuse. In one study, a little over 12 percent of parents of infants six months old and younger confessed that they had hit or shaken their babies at least one time on account of their infants' crying. The parents participating in the study cited their belief that the crying was excessive as the primary factor for having lost control of their anger. It may be that the parents' own needs had not been getting met, and their child's crying triggered feelings in them that they did not express.

Some children seem to clamor constantly for parents to give them attention. Others feel envious and become angry with parents when they give attention to each other, and accuse the parents of ignoring them. You may notice that a demanding child's siblings don't require as much attention and become resentful that the more attention the parent gives the demanding child, the more the child seems to want. It doesn't seem fair.

In the early chapters of this book I emphasized that anger is caused when something feels unfair. It seems natural, then, that you may feel angry with a child who wants so much. When parents have an unhealthy relationship with anger that they are carrying over from their own childhood, they are unable to express these feelings and to set appropriate boundaries with their own child. When mixed with a predisposition for aggression, parents' inability to manage their anger puts them in greater danger of engaging in corporal punishment and child abuse. Abused children continue the unhealthy pattern, behaving in the way that their parents modeled, and yet another generation is deprived of the opportunity to learn how to express anger and frustration productively. Aggression is passed on — from the generation who hits to the generation who is hit.

Sometimes parental anger is provoked by worry. When your child crosses the street without looking, you may get angry with her. You still love her; your anger co-exists with the love. This experience of anger illustrates how it can serve as a signal that a change needs to take place. The change in this case would be either for you to supervise your child more closely when she crosses the street or for you to teach her the importance of looking both ways before she steps out into the street. Your anger here provides an opportunity for your child not only to learn an important lesson that might some day save her life but also one that demonstrates how to express anger respectfully and effectively.

At other times, your anger may be provoked when your child does not follow the rules you set at home. For example, if you want him to get up at a certain time in order to get to school on time and he ignores you or refuses to comply, you will probably feel angry. He may feel angry over being told what to do and when to do it. If you do not express your feelings, you are more likely to act out your anger. Likewise, when you refuse to allow your child to express his anger in turn, he will most likely find aggressive or passive-aggressive ways to act it out, through temper tantrums, rudeness, or silent defiance.

If you were raised in a family where anger was an emotion that was to be controlled, you may disapprove of your own child's expressions of anger and attempt to censor her angry words. Your child will eventually conclude that anger is a bad, disgraceful part of herself and revealing it will get her in trouble. After a while, all uncomfortable emotions and less-than-perfect behavior become shameful in your child's mind. In order to preserve her sense of self-worth, she may begin to take control by obsessively worrying about being "nice," rather than risk the appearance of being out of control or unacceptable in any way. I have seen adult clients whose therapy primarily involved resolving shame and self-blame and allowing themselves to feel and express anger and its underlying feelings without self-reproach.

The cost of anger in a child's life should not be underestimated. Studies have verified that hostile parents leave their children emotionally scarred. When parents act out in anger toward their child, the child loses his sense that he is worthy of receiving love and care from anyone, and he becomes insecure. This loss of security can lead to obedience problems and create additional conflict between the parent and the child. The cycle of acting out continues because neither the parent nor the child has mastered the ability to manage their behavior when they don't get what is needed or wanted. This is the parent-child loop, similar to the partner loop I described earlier:

Parent calls child a name
or otherwise belittles the child...   Child throws a tantrum...

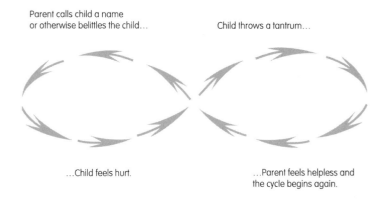

...Child feels hurt.   ...Parent feels helpless and
                                                        the cycle begins again.

Illustration 4: Parent-Child Loop

The only way out of the loop is for you to stop acting out through belittling or shaming your child and to let him know that *he* is loved, anger and all, but his *acting-out behavior* is not.

If you are a parent and you get angry, identify who or what you're angry at. Some parents are jealous of their children for reasons that relate back to their own childhood. For example, if you were always jealous of your talented big sister, is that old jealousy coming out in angry disapproval of your daughter who resembles her? You may be lonely, unhappy, depressed and under enormous stress. You may have problems that adversely affect your ability to deal with your children. You may even be angry about having to raise your children, resentful over having to be the person that your children rely on day after day. Clients have told me that their mothers became angry with them for being sick. Perhaps they were not really angry at their children but at the situation. Nevertheless, their indirect anger affected their children. It always does.

ANGER POINTS

• Arrival of children can compound a relationship that is already troubled with anger and resentment.

• Neglecting your own needs can trigger anger at your child's demands.

• Generations who hit pass the pattern of aggression down to the following generation.

• Expressing your anger respectfully and effectively can serve as role modeling for your child.

• Reproaching your child for expressing her anger can cause her to feel shame and self-blame.

8

And What About Other Relationships?

It's a fact that people are going to be angry with you from time to time. Sometimes it will be through no fault of your own. People can act unreasonably toward the nearest target — and that will be you! Because their treatment feels unfair, you will feel angry in return. At other times they will trigger your anger through words or actions specifically directed at you because of something you have done or not done. You have a choice in these situations. Your choice is either to accept the other's anger and express your own feelings or to act them out.

In therapy, I support my clients' efforts to address their anger at me honestly and openly. When clients have been angry with me, it has most often been over my expectation that they adhere to my 24-hour cancellation policy. Their underlying thought in these situations is that my policy is not fair to them. As I have studied the emotion of anger, it has become clear to me how our own feeling of unfairness blinds us from considering the degree of fairness to the other person. I recall clients who have argued that they should not have to pay for a late cancelled session because they had, after all, let me know a few hours before the session that they would not be keeping their appointments. Their own feeling of unfairness blinded them to the fact that it would be unfair to *me* not to get paid for a session that I had little likelihood of filling due to the late notice. In each case, it is not until I accept their anger and empathize with their feeling of unfairness that they are able to hear *my* perspective, and we are able to repair the rupture that has occurred. Once the repair takes place, we continue to work on issues that are important to them, and occasionally we refer back to how angry they had been in that earlier session. It becomes a part of their healing process in therapy. If they were to choose to keep their anger to themselves or if I were to become defensive and ignore how my action affected them, or cause them to feel guilty or as if there were something wrong with them for expressing anger at me, they might leave therapy and we would lose the opportunity to use the rupture and repair as tools for their healing.

What's important in these situations is to avoid getting into the loop when someone sees only her own side of the picture. It seems to be human nature to focus on our own sense of unfairness and respond accordingly. If you do this, however, you will most likely damage relationships. My own experience has taught me to step out of the loop and to receive the other person's expression of anger. The other person needs to be heard. The person needs to hear that you acknowledge the anger and to know that you accept it, and that you will not close her out because of it.

Anger is a cry to be heard. It needs to be listened to. Choosing to receive another's anger requires that you pay full attention to it. If you listen to it, you offer respect to it. It is often said that anger is a secondary emotion because other emotions lie beneath it. In paying attention to the anger, you may also be able to recognize the feelings that underlie the anger. In order to succeed in managing your anger, you must become skillful at identifying and expressing the underlying feelings. However, when you don't even pay attention to the secondary feeling of anger, the primary level of feelings is neglected as well.

ANGER POINTS

- **A**ll of us are targets of anger at one time or another.

- **N**oting the other person's perspective enables you to empathize with him rather than defending your own position.

- **G**etting into the loop does damage to a relationship.

- **E**veryone needs to be heard.

- **R**especting the other person's anger requires that you give it your full attention.

9

Oh, The Things Those Very Angry People Do— Binge-Eating, Workaholism, Obsessive-Compulsive Behavior, Phobias, Road Rage, and Miscellaneous Health Effects of Anger

When anger is inhibited, suppressed or repressed, a variety of emotional disorders can result. If you view anger as a shameful feeling, you may act it out through compulsive behavior or obsessive thoughts, or show other symptoms of anxiety, such as phobias. When you cannot allow yourself to feel your own anger and to express it effectively, you may release your frustration through eating, work, sex, shopping, gambling, drinking or the use of drugs. These activities may initially serve as a diversion from allowing yourself to accept and feel the intensity of your anger, but when used for this purpose they are addictive. As addictions grow, particularly addictions to drugs and alcohol, over time they tend to fuel a person's anger rather than simply diverting it. It's easy to imagine this escalation of anger in the case of substance addiction because, for example, people who are addicted to alcohol or drugs have been known to fly into a rage when they drink or use. The escalation of anger tends to be more subtle as a person digs himself more deeply into eating, shopping, gambling or other addictive behaviors. Nevertheless, over time his anger grows.

Overeating and Workaholism

Overeating and workaholism seem to have become commonplace in our society. Both are self-defeating behaviors. Like depression, they are forms of anger that are turned inward and buried deep inside. Overeaters and workaholics are often trying to avoid emotional pain through immediate gratification. Their relationships do not feel supportive or nurturing. Rather than expressing anger over the lack of support or nurture, their methods of coping may be to wrap their anger in the fat that armors them in an effort to keep people at a distance or to escape it through their work.[8] Either way, they deprive their partners and themselves of closeness and intimacy. If they don't pay attention to their feelings and consequently reject their own anger, then they and their partner become skilled at distancing from feelings. Workaholics often do not feel genuine emotion. In fact, their real emotions are closed off. Alienating and closing off others prevents bonding, sharing and a mutually loving relationship. People then find themselves in relationships that feel uncaring and cold.

Obsessions, Compulsions and Phobias

Anger is often a factor in obsessions, compulsions and phobias. Obsessions are constant disturbing irrational *thoughts* that people can't get out of their heads. The tape plays over and over. A compulsion is a ritualistic *action* that a person feels compelled to do over and over again. Rather than expressing their anger directly, these people often express their anger inwardly at themselves through obsessive thoughts or compulsive acts. Phobias, or fears of specific things or situations, may also result from pent-up anger. When you conceal anger, it may surface where you least expect it. Unexpressed anger can be replaced by anxiety or panic attacks. A vicious cycle is created: you do not allow yourself to feel or express your anger, the anger shows itself in the form of worry, the worry causes you to misinterpret the actions of others, you do not allow yourself to feel or express your anger…and so on, and so on, and so on.

Road Rage

Whatever you do when your anger is out of control is not going to be done well. Road rage is a phenomenon that has been reported increasingly in the news. Let's face it; driving is stressful on today's roadways. More and more, drivers lead frenzied and fast-paced lives that create pressure and anxiety. When a person is already feeling angry or frustrated by problems at work or at home, it doesn't take much to put him "over the edge" while driving. Psychologists use the term "road rage" to describe the hostility that drivers feel behind the wheel that causes them to retaliate in some way against other drivers. The American Automobile Association Foundation for Traffic Safety estimates that reported road rage incidents are increasing by a rate of seven percent each year. Unfortunately, a driver with road rage is headed for disaster — for himself and for the other drivers on the road.

Health Effects

Anger has both immediate and lasting effects on your physical and emotional well being. If you don't understand how to deal with your anger, it can destroy you. You become a casualty of your own anger. It causes distress to your entire body, producing physical and emotional strain within you. When you feel angry, your heart rate and blood pressure rise, along with levels of certain hormones, particularly adrenaline and noradrenaline. If you hold your anger in, over time your physiological reactions can lead to physical illness. Anger that is harbored within can actually be toxic to your body, causing heart disease and other stress-related illness. The same is true of explosive anger. Both pent-up and explosive anger have physiologically damaging effects.

Research has revealed that men in particular who have poor anger management skills are more likely to suffer a heart attack before age 55 than those who can express their anger in a less volatile manner. Apparently the presence of C-reactive protein in the blood indicates inflammation of the arteries. It has been found that those who are prone to anger, hostility or depression have blood levels of C-reactive protein that are two or three times higher than those who do not display those characteristics. The conclusion drawn is that anger is a predictor of increased heart disease risk in otherwise healthy individuals. This implies that learning to manage anger might prevent heart disease. As for women who deal with their anger by suppressing it, those who withdraw and are unable to discuss their anger are at higher risk of heart disease than their counterparts who express their anger effectively. The results of this research provide ample reason for changing the way you deal with your anger.

ANGER POINTS

- **A**ddictive behaviors tend to fuel your anger over time rather than merely diverting it.

- **N**urture and support are often absent from the lives of people who overeat and overwork.

- **G**oing over and over a particular situation in your head rather than expressing your anger directly leads to obsessions, compulsions and phobias.

- **E**motional well being is necessary for your overall health.

- **R**oad rage is caused by people who do not manage their stress and anxiety in a healthy way.

10

Why Does It Have to Happen to Me?
Aging and Illness

The causes of anger vary at different stages of your life. As you get older, if you continually fail to acknowledge the source of your anger, the risk increases that you will take it out on the people around you. Many people in their seventies and eighties were taught to "grin and bear it" and are not comfortable talking about their feelings. If you never allow yourself to feel your emotions and talk about them, by the time you get to your seventies and eighties you will have a lifetime of negative feelings stored deep inside.

Those who spend time with seriously ill people often witness episodes of intense anger, sometimes even when the threat of the illness has passed. In fact, the aftermath of any life-threatening illness can be more challenging than the treatment of the illness itself. A person may need to grieve the loss of how life used to be before she can move forward. While the person is in the throes of diagnosis and treatment, she may stuff the difficult emotions. But stuffed emotions tend to resurface. One of the emotions that usually resurfaces is grief.

Our society's approach to grief and loss has changed over the past forty years. We have come to recognize that anger is part of the grieving process, regardless of what or who it is we have lost. The most common losses experienced by an older person are the loss of the person he was — his youth, his physical fitness and his attraction; the loss of his employment-related identity and financial security through retirement; the loss of friends and family through illness and death; and the loss of experiences he always dreamed of but will never have.

It is natural for you to grieve losses, particularly immediately after the realization of a specific loss sets in. Freedom is one of the most fundamental psychological emotional needs. When your freedom is lost or restricted, you become angry. A person may perceive each setback as an indication that God or fate is singling him out. (Theoretically, he is angry at the unfairness of the circumstances. If he follows a religion, he's angry with his God.) He may develop a "victim mindset." This feeling of victimization makes him angry as well. This can cause him to suffer emotionally as well as physically. He holds the belief that life should be fair and that life is fair to others but not to him. Feeling that he is being treated unfairly increases the anger. If you've ever visited a sick friend in a hospital, you may have noticed that you are sympathetic to expressions of sadness or fear but grow uneasy when a sick person voices anger. Perceiving their guest's uneasiness, patients are inclined to conceal their anger and attempt to fill up quiet moments with cheerful chatter, despite their feeling anything but cheerful.

But anger is a normal coping mechanism in the process of coming to terms with loss. It serves an important function. If you do not allow yourself to experience anger during grieving, your ability to move beyond the grief and to heal will be impaired. Expressing anger may actually be healthier for you than resigning to the loss quietly. Quiet resignation causes you to stuff the anger. Expressing it enables you to get it out so that you can move beyond it. This is why grief counselors initially explore a person's degree of anger and encourage the release of these feelings. During the incident of loss, there is usually no place for a person to express or even acknowledge that she is angry. Yet, it is normal to feel angry over loss.

Sometimes after experiencing a loss a person will act out his grief by failing to take care of himself, isolating himself from friends and other family members, or refusing to return to a "normal" life. He turns irritable and family and friends want to avoid him. Not only does he lose the people and things that were important to him but his behavior alienates him also from the support system that remains. This behavior is a form of acting out of unresolved anger.

Expressing angry feelings helps family and friends to understand what you need. Letting the anger out may relieve your sadness or fear. Even at this time it may be possible to use your anger constructively.

ANGER POINTS

• **A**llowing yourself to feel your emotions and talk about them prevents you from storing up a lifetime of negative feelings deep inside yourself.

• **N**eeding to grieve the loss of how life used to be is natural as you move from one stage of life to another.

• **G**rief involves anger.

• **E**xpressions of anger are often concealed by those who are ill to dispel the uneasiness of those who are healthy.

• **R**efusing to return to a normal routine after a significant loss may indicate the presence of unresolved anger.

Part Two

Putting Your Best Anger Forward

11

If My Anger Isn't Working, How Can I Fix It?

Perhaps you've surmised by now that among the clients I work with I have noticed that the single most damaging factor in their lives is not their anger but their inability to acknowledge and express it. Mental health clinics and therapists' practices are filled with people who do not know how to express their anger effectively. Anger that is not expressed can lead to low self-esteem, anxiety, depression and aggressive behavior.

I suggest a six-step process toward expressing anger effectively:

- Develop a better understanding of it.
- Acknowledge that anger has benefits.
- Make a distinction between productive and non-productive anger.
- Accept the anger in yourself. This step may require "accepting the unacceptable."
- Find ways to express your anger respectfully and productively.
- Find ways to accept another's anger respectfully and productively. Refrain from thinking that it's "not okay" to be angry and from telling yourself or another *not* to be angry.

Let's look at each of these steps in more detail.

Developing a Better Understanding of Anger
That's what this book is all about. Anger is a healthy and positive feeling that helps you to convey to another person that

you have uncomfortable feelings about something or that you feel mistreated in some way. Anger that is harmful and destructive crosses over the line from anger to rage, hostility or bitterness (inward hostility). Bitterness is old anger that lies under the surface, waiting to erupt when it's least expected. It continues to build up within you as long as the problems causing the anger remain unaddressed, and it usually leads to depression. When working with a depressed client, one of the initial questions I ask is, "Have you been unable to tell people in your life how much they have hurt you?"

A Young Man Learns

There's a wonderful metaphor for suppressed anger in the old Welsh and Irish legend of the Fisher King. Briefly, one version of the story goes like this:

A young man sets out for home after his adventures with the Knights of King Arthur. On his way he gets lost and meets up with an old fisherman. The fisherman gives him directions to his own house, which the young man discovers is a castle. He is welcomed inside to join in a great feast. The fisherman tells the young man that he was once a king, but a wound in his leg that will not heal restricts his activities, and so he passes the time by fishing. As they dine, a procession of young people passes by. The young people are carrying a variety of interesting objects. Although the young man wonders about the significance of the objects, he says nothing. The next morning he awakens to find the castle empty. He wanders into the forest and meets a maiden who tells him that his failure to express his thoughts and feelings about what he saw in the procession has placed the kingdom at risk. In an effort to correct his mistake, the young man sets out again in search of the castle and becomes lost. After five years' time, he finally comes upon the Fisher King's castle. Again, he is welcomed inside to a feast. Again, a procession of young people carrying a variety of interesting objects passes before him and the Fisher King as they eat. This time the young man expresses what is on his mind about what he is seeing. When he does, his questions are answered, the King's wound heals, and the kingdom is no longer at risk.

This story can serve as a guide for examining the way you deal with your anger. How many hurts have you held onto, rather than expressing your thoughts or feelings about what you have experienced? To what extent does your failure to talk about your anger, and your harboring of bitterness, put your relationships (your kingdoms) at risk? Bitter people tend to blame others for having caused them pain, but hold their feelings inside. I have worked with clients who failed to respond to family members' behavior that made them uncomfortable. Not only did they hide their anger, but in most cases the unexpressed anger fomented into bitterness. Like the young man in the Fisher King legend, their silence put their kingdoms at risk. Just as the young man wandered for five years before finding the castle again, perhaps you have spent many years trying to find the key to expressing your anger.

Because you are human, you become angry from time to time. However, the degree to which you are comfortable with your anger differs from that of the person next to you. As I've shown earlier, how you cope with your anger when it arises is related to how negative feelings were expressed in your family when you were a child — whether negative feelings were expressed at all and, if so, how those feelings were expressed. If your family did not acknowledge anger, you are likely to have problems allowing yourself to feel your anger. You may not even notice when others are treating you unfairly because denying or ignoring the unfair treatment is preferable to addressing it. You may become entrapped in the belief that anger is disgraceful. You may be slow to become aware of your personal anger symptoms, and may not feel your anger until it is upon you — if indeed you feel it at all. Because you were not afforded the opportunity during your childhood to practice expressing your anger in a healthy way, you most likely either "stuff it" (like the young man in the Fisher King legend) or explode inappropriately. Remember, however, that even "stuffed" anger surfaces later when you least expect it.

Acknowledging That Anger Has Benefits
     This is a good place to talk about the two types of healthy anger: collective anger and personal anger.

Collective Anger
     Collective anger is the anger that is felt by a group of people in connection with a common cause. This type of anger plays an important role in society. History is filled with stories of how anger — the feeling of being "fed up" — served as an agent for change. Anger can turn what is unfair into something that is fair. It is healthy to feel collective anger and to use it to counter unfairness and create ways to bring about reform. Collective anger enables us as members of a society to express our common negative feelings and correct an injustice. The act of reflecting upon unfairness and discussing it with others may produce constructive results. Examples of the productive application of anger by collective groups can be seen in the activities of organizations like People for the Ethical Treatment of Animals (PETA); trade unions, e.g., the International Brotherhood of Teamsters and the AFL-CIO; and Greenpeace, the organization that pushes for environmental change. When these groups see what they perceive to be an injustice, they rally their members to effect change. Another example of collective anger was displayed upon the death of Pope John Paul II. Politicians in France argued over whether the French government had abused its powers by lowering the flags on state buildings as a tribute to the late Pope. Left-wing groups saw it as a violation of the country's strict century-old separation of church and state. They felt strongly about the issue, and they expressed their convictions. They shared a collective anger.[9]
     Unfortunately, collective anger can go awry. A prime example is collective anger that is based on prejudice. Prejudice is a judgment about a person or group that is founded on preconceptions and overgeneralizations. When people

express prejudice in the form of critical remarks, they create a one-up/one-down situation. Prejudice leads to discrimination. Discrimination causes the person or group that is discriminated against to feel angry and sometimes hostile. The collective anger of those who discriminate begets the collective anger of those who are discriminated against. It's a lose-lose situation.

Personal Anger

Personal anger occurs when we or those close to us have been hurt. There are cases where medical doctors misdiagnose or administer the wrong dosage of medication, sometimes with fatal results. The family's anger at these doctors is an example of personal anger. The same event can evoke both personal and collective anger: personal anger is felt by those whose lives have been directly affected, and collective anger can be felt by those who hear about it and express their anger in the form of public outcry. Whether anger is collective or personal, it can be beneficial. It has the following potential:

• To be adaptive and creative. It is adaptive when it helps you to respond to a threat at hand. It is creative when it helps you to solve problems, because it can serve as fuel for your imagination. Healthy anger has value when it motivates you to discover solutions and to seek compromise. If you put your creative powers to use, you can actually have something to show for feeling angry.

• To let you know that it's time for a change. Anger is a sign that something needs to be done, although you may not yet know what you want to do about a situation. It can be a catalyst for bringing about change. Recall the rage of Demeter (see Chapter 4). It gave her the momentum for bringing Persephone back from the Underworld. Anger can provide you with a chart that shows you where your limits are, or where you want to go. Anger can be your ally or adversary. It depends on how you decide to communicate it. Sometimes you may feel like pointing a finger at someone in blame. That's a shortsighted behavior. If you look beyond the person you'd like to blame, your anger can point in the direction you need to go to solve the situation.

• To be user-friendly. If you use your anger in a healthy way, it is your ally, not your adversary. It is your ally when you use it thoughtfully to achieve a particular objective. Understanding how to acknowledge and communicate your anger appropriately can make it easier for you to attain your objectives, work out difficulties and manage crises. Failure to acknowledge and comprehend your anger can cause a range of problems. What may be helpful for you to remember is that angry feelings can help you to bring about change, but the actions necessary for change need not be angry actions. When you manage angry feelings effectively, they help you to undertake non-angry actions. When used in this way, anger is a tool, not the end product.

• To give you a sense of control over what happens. Anger provides a feeling of agency and power. Sometimes you may have to employ your own power in order to challenge the power of others. It can help you to be firm. It can motivate action. During this process, changes take place.

• To heal what hurts you. It helps you to speak your experience, and speaking about your experience is the first step toward healing.

Making a Distinction Between Productive and Non-Productive Anger

There is useful anger and anger that is not useful. It's important to gain a sense of when to express anger and when to keep quiet. There are times when expressing anger is quite appropriate. Healthy, positive anger does not damage a relationship. Anger is effective when you direct it only at the person who has offended you. But you may have never learned to state your angry feelings in an effective way. For the most part you may have discovered ways of dealing with anger by accident and without much straightforward training. You may lack the skills necessary to feel secure expressing your negative feelings. When I begin working with a client who wants to work specifically on anger, I find that the person has come to think that all manifestation of anger is wrong and that she should not be expressing it at all. She soon learns that it is not wrong to *feel* angry and to express it but that it is wrong to express it or act it out in a destructive way. And so she begins to draw a distinction between speaking about her anger and acting it out.

When you don't know the language of anger, it comes out in negative tones and creates problems in relationships at home, in the workplace and in other areas of your life. When you have acquired anger skills by chance, you may have become skilled at being aggressive or violent as your immediate reaction to anger and its associated stress. Or you may have discovered how to stuff, play down or disown your anger. In place of anger, you may suffer depression, hurt, extreme guilt or shame. You may have yourself convinced that you never feel angry. Or you may think that managing anger is a sign of weakness.

Healthy, productive anger is reasonable and feels within bounds. You make a choice not to engage in out-of-control behavior when you are faced with a challenging situation. It conveys a general feeling of respect for the other person, even though you may feel angry with him. In an intimate relationship, expressing anger constructively and peacefully can feel almost sacred because it honors the affectionate bond between you and does not destroy it. Although you might like to see your partner behave differently, you still feel affection for him, despite your feeling angry. After healthy anger is expressed, you can let go of the anger and feel at ease once more.

If you were to sit back and objectively observe the process of healthy anger, what you would notice would most likely be a sequence of steps beginning with the initial symptoms and ending with the actions chosen to resolve it. It might look something like the diagram on the next page. As you can see, in order to resolve anger, you must regain the emotional stability of Stage IV.

It's important to distinguish between productive and non-

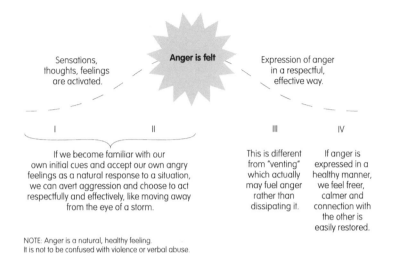

Anger is felt

Sensations, thoughts, feelings are activated.

Expression of anger in a respectful, effective way.

I	II	III	IV

If we become familiar with our own initial cues and accept our own angry feelings as a natural response to a situation, we can avert aggression and choose to act respectfully and effectively, like moving away from the eye of a storm.

This is different from "venting" which actually may fuel anger rather than dissipating it.

If anger is expressed in a healthy manner, we feel freer, calmer and connection with the other is easily restored.

NOTE: Anger is a natural, healthy feeling.
It is not to be confused with violence or verbal abuse.

Illustration 5: The Process of Healthy Anger

productive anger because anger in general is most likely the most inadequately managed emotion today. Destructive anger is widespread in our current culture, as filled as it is with pressures of all kinds. The development of cell phones and other electronic communication devices now enables rageful people to explode spontaneously at their targets. Reacting spontaneously in anger is usually destructive. Destructive anger creates obstacles in your life and destroys relationships. If your anger is out of control, you are likely to misperceive another person's communication and jump to the wrong conclusions about the other person's thoughts and motives. You will "go for the jugular," attacking the other in her most vulnerable places. These attacks tend to evoke an equally harmful response from the other person. Once this destructive process begins, it spreads like an uncontained forest fire. Your thoughts become distorted and illogical. Acting-out behaviors and aggression follow. More often than not, the outcome of destructive anger is separation, estrangement and loneliness.

It is destructive anger — the type that is non-productive — that causes the media and society to give anger in general a bad rap. We open the newspaper or turn on the news to hear countless stories and view disturbing images of hostility, aggression and peoples' mistreatment of others. We read about cruelty to people and animals, destruction of property, the breakup of relationships, campaigns of terror against targeted groups of people, and combat between countries. Even our favorite celebrities are ordered by courts to undergo anger management therapy. Anger is portrayed as bad. We don't hear many stories about people who express their anger in healthy, productive ways.

Unhealthy, destructive anger is addictive. An anger addict gets caught up in the conviction that his feelings are always justified. Someone acts foolishly, and the anger addict feels justified to be angry. And so the cycle of constant anger begins. Like any addiction, destructive anger may result in feelings of guilt and may even result in physical harm. Addictive anger can consume your life. It is chronic and never ends. As quickly and easily as an addictive substance, addictive anger can destroy relationships between husbands and wives, brothers and sisters, kids in school and adults in the workplace.

Accepting the Anger in Yourself

How well can you tolerate your own anger? Become familiar with the anger in yourself. You may refuse to allow yourself to experience anger. You may believe you are not entitled to be angry, especially if the person to whom your anger is directed has treated you well in the past. You may tell yourself you "should not" feel angry. In fact, you may strongly believe in general that no one should ever become angry.

I have worked with clients who described their parents and siblings as all extremely peaceful, never becoming angry. These clients cannot understand why they themselves feel angry and view their own feelings as "wrong." As we explore their childhoods, they recall that they hid their anger and suffered hurts and disappointments in silence. They and their entire families denied feelings and held them in rather than expressing them. If these families had dealt with their anger constructively, these clients may have developed acceptance of their anger and the anger of others.

You have a choice whether to disown your anger and keep it hidden inside or to allow yourself to feel it and react to it in a constructive way. You may disclaim your anger by apologizing for it and saying, "I don't know what came over me." This makes it sound as though the anger is separate from you. Viewing it in this way will prevent you from managing it. You cannot manage what you disown. If you embrace it rather than distance from it, you will soon experience less shame and regret over feeling your anger. After all, anger is a natural emotion. The reason it's important to accept your own anger is that anger and irritations occur during the course of everyday life. It is unreasonable to expect that you can interact with other people without ever getting angry. If you don't accept your own anger, you will berate yourself for it or blame it on others. If you acknowledge your feelings and accept them as natural, you begin to realize that feelings just "are." You don't need to feel bad about them or blame others for them. Honestly stating "I feel angry" indicates that you own your feeling and that you recognize that you have a choice as to how you will respond to it. Furthermore, if you embrace your anger you will be able to observe its source. This insight in itself can help you to resolve a situation.

Finding Ways to Express Your Anger Respectfully and Productively

You may lack the skills needed to express your angry feelings constructively and respectfully to the person you're angry at, and so you act in a way that adversely affects yourself and others: you conceal your anger inside because it feels like the safer thing to do. This concealment can lead to psychological and physical problems. Freud believed that internalized anger caused depression. Here's how it works. If you were brought up with the idea that it is not okay to be angry, you may suppress your anger. You may fear that if you do express it, others will respond negatively to you. You may believe that if the significant people in your life respond negatively, they will not like you and will reject you. You may not be able to bear the thought that a person who is important to you feels negatively toward you, if only for a moment. Therefore, you may feel the need to act in a way that will sustain the approval of that important person. You may reason that you can't be angry with someone you need in your life. When you think this way, you make the assumption that anger of any type, healthy or unhealthy, drives others away. This way of thinking also reinforces the idea that anger is not okay and that something is wrong with you if you are angry.

People tend to react to anger in one of four ways:

• They stuff it. Often children receive praise when they display positive emotions and are scolded or told to "get over it" when they display negative emotions. If this was your experience as a child, it's no wonder that as you grew up you may have developed the belief that anger is something to be avoided at all costs. The problem is that stuffed anger doesn't go away. It continues to brew deep inside and often leaks out in subtle, passive-aggressive ways. Forcing yourself to bottle up your anger reduces your self-respect because it invalidates your own experience. When you're conscious of your anger and get down on yourself for feeling it, you are devaluing your own feeling. When anger is devalued and not accepted as a normal emotion, if you ever do express anger to a loved one, you may view yourself as bad. You may end up pointing your anger inwardly, aiming it at yourself, and eventually disliking yourself for being angry.

• They try to express it, but it comes out awkwardly. Even when you are accustomed to stuffing your anger, eventually you may get up enough nerve to "speak up for yourself," but your words may be ineffective because you have never learned the language of anger. You may have heard that it is good to express your feelings, and so you try, but you may use words and a tone of voice that don't accomplish what you intended and may even have a hurtful impact on your loved ones. If you are not accustomed to expressing your anger, initially it will feel unfamiliar and awkward. Emotionally, you may be like an infant or toddler. But it's like learning anything. Emotional development takes some time. When you allow yourself to begin to express your anger, your expressions of anger may initially seem like outbursts. These outbursts can be disconcerting and may cause you to question whether you truly want to learn how to express your anger. As you become more tolerant of your own angry feelings, you expand your ability to express it in respectful ways.

• They explode. Everyone knows people like this. Their reaction is analogous to swatting a fly with a sledgehammer. Not only is the fly destroyed but so is the shelf upon which it was standing! These people seem to get unreasonably angry at relatively minor annoyances. What is actually happening is that many, many minor things have accumulated over time, creating a major mountain of minor irritations. Then comes the "last straw" and a torrent of anger is unleashed, much of which has nothing to do with the person toward whom it is directed. The people in this group often begin to fear their own rage. Let's imagine that your body is a container for all of your emotions, pleasant and unpleasant. But when you don't express your anger, it's like putting an airtight lid on the container. The anger swirls around inside you but it has nowhere to go. Each time you feel angry the pressure builds until finally the container can't hold anymore and the lid blows off. You may call it "blowing your top" or "letting off steam."

• A small minority of people can express their anger effectively. Either they grew up in an uncommon family environment where these skills were taught and practiced, or more likely, they have acquired them along the way through counseling or other personal growth work. They know how to express their anger and receive it from others in a respectful, non-hurtful way. Keep in mind that the first step for the people in this category was to accept their own anger as a natural human emotion and then manage it accordingly. You can do this, too. To follow the example of the container with a stopper, imagine that you release the stopper ever so slightly, so that you feel a soft "swoosh" as the feeling escapes. By staying current and removing the stopper in a managed way, you avoid either potentially exploding or allowing your anger to foment inside.

Finding Ways to Accept Another's Anger Respectfully and Productively

One way to accept another person's anger is to try to understand her perspective. In the face of another's anger, it's easy to convince yourself that the other person is wrong. However, when you look at the situation through her lens, you may be astonished to discover that she's not as unreasonable as she seemed. You may then be able to appreciate why she responded as she did. You may even find that the judgments you had made, or the motives you had ascribed to her behavior, were not valid.

ANGER POINTS

- **A**ggression and low self-esteem develop when anger is not expressed.

- **N**eglecting your feelings puts the quality of your life and your relationships at risk.

- **G**roup anger can bring about needed change (constructive) or create hateful situations (destructive).

- **E**lectronic devices are convenient and fast, but communicating your anger before taking time to consider whether and how to express it poses a hazard to your relationship.

- **R**enouncing your anger robs you of the choice as to how to deal with it.

12

I Remember a Time When...: Your Personal Anger History and Your Present-Day Anger

What experiences do you recall from childhood that caused you to feel angry? If you cannot remember ever being angry as a child, you may be dissociating from the memories and suppressing all recollection of the experience. It may have been taboo to be angry, or anger may have been viewed as a weakness. If it wasn't okay to even feel angry, you may have worked very hard to disown any memory of the times you did feel it. However, if you can, recall a time during childhood when you were angry. Write down a short account of the circumstances. Try to remember the situations that regularly made you angry. Perhaps you were treated differently from your siblings, or your parents never allowed you to be who you truly were. As you remember those events, notice what comes to mind: the tones of voice, gestures and words that you or others used. Was there any verbal abuse such as blaming, name-calling, threats or shouting? Did you experience or witness physical violence? Whatever it was, bring it to mind.

Now recall how you as a child responded to the circumstances that come to mind. Recalling your early experience may help you to understand more clearly why you react to anger the way you do today. Take your time thinking and writing about the past. Do you still respond in the same way to similar situations, or has your response changed over time since you were a child? The more aware you become of your history with anger and its connection to your current life, the better equipped you will be to change the way you respond to others today. Once you have spent some thinking about your history of anger, shift to the present and consider whether you are retaining residual effects from your early experience with anger. When you become angry today, do you keep it to yourself or do you show it openly? How so? If you express it openly, do you stick to talking about your own experience, or do you attack others by putting them down or using sarcasm? Do you "lose your cool" with impulsive outbursts, reacting too quickly to pause and consider the circumstances calmly? Become mindful of the intensity of your anger. If you were to rate your typical anger level on a scale of 1 to 10, with 1 being low intensity and 10 being high intensity, where does it fall?

Your automatic response may be to lash out aggressively. Think of the times you have used this technique and try to recall the consequences. Impulsively lashing out may provide temporary relief but brings damaging results. It prevents you from truthfully owning your feelings and turns you into a verbal abuser. Expressing hostile feelings by impulsively raging or criticizing others only hurts the other person and may make you feel remorseful and embarrassed later.

You may find that you neither act aggressively nor express your anger directly. If so, you are at risk of acting passive-aggressively. In passive-aggressive behavior, a person appears to agree with the wishes or demands of others but in fact passively defies them. This passive defiance is a form of aggression, hence the term *passive-aggression*. You may be extremely skilled at expressing anger in this way. When you are passive-aggressive, you may be moody, distant and obsessed with the fact that you've been hurt, but you don't ever talk about your hurt! Instead, you focus on everything that's wrong with the situation, the other person or the relationship. And still you remain silent. As you sulk in silence, you become more and more entrenched in your anger and you begin to express it subtly. You may do things to get even: criticize, spread rumors, glare, pout or stonewall the people around you.[10] Because you do not acknowledge straightforwardly how you feel, you conceal your anger and act it out subtly. Sometimes people feel coerced into passive aggression because they fear others' reactions to their direct expressions of anger. Ironically, passive aggressors themselves often cause the people around them to feel guilty for expressing anger directly. If you find that someone around you frequently displays passive-aggressive behavior, ask yourself whether you are inhibiting her straightforward expression of anger, and in so doing, driving her to express the anger passively.

As you think about your present relationship with anger, take into account what happens internally, both physically and emotionally, when you are angry. Do you feel as though you've been knocked off balance? Where do you feel the anger — in your chest, in your stomach, or elsewhere in your body? Does anger distress you? Are you angry *that* you feel angry? Perhaps you feel like crying when you get angry.

What is it like to allow yourself to explore your anger in this way? It's normal to feel a bit uncomfortable at this point in the book. Anger is not a pleasant emotion, and thinking about how you mismanage your anger is equally unpleasant. But you have completed an important step, which is increasing your awareness of how you "do" anger. Awareness is key to changing any behavior.

ANGER POINTS

- **A**cknowledging your anger history prepares you to change your current anger behavior.

- **N**umerically rating your typical anger level from 1 to 10 gives you a reading of its intensity.

- **G**oing silent with your anger but acting it out in subtle ways is passive-aggressive.

- **E**xploring your physical and emotional experience of anger is key to changing how you behave when you are angry.

- **R**emorse and embarrassment often follow impulsive outbursts of anger.

13

*One Potato, Two Potato: Choosing Whether
and When to Express Your Anger*

People have told me that they had "no choice" but to act out their anger in particular situations. It's not true that they had no choice. They simply did not recognize that they actually had two additional choices: (1) to feel their anger and express it constructively or (2) to feel it and refrain from expressing it. Imagine a world in which each of us went around expressing our anger in every situation!

There's a difference between feeling anger and expressing it. It's always good to allow yourself to feel your anger. It's not always a good idea to express it in the moment. Whether or not you express it, and when to express it, are separate questions. Timing and circumstances are the determining factors. You need to weigh which are greater, the advantages or disadvantages of expressing your anger. If the advantages carry more weight than the disadvantages, go right ahead and express how you feel. Failing to do so at those times is a denial of what you believe is right or of what you need. Bottling up this anger can ultimately harm you. Remember, one of your goals is to find a way in which you can use your voice to express anger so that the pressure inside the container is released before the container explodes.

If the disadvantages outweigh the advantages, think twice before you say anything. While it may benefit you in the short run because it offers a cathartic release of your feelings, expressing it may have adverse long-term effects. I am not suggesting that you stuff your anger and pretend that it is not there. Choosing to let go of anger and not express it is different from pretending that you don't feel it. As harmful as it might be to express anger at the wrong time and in the wrong place, it is just as harmful to ignore the feeling completely. The difference between choosing not to express anger and suppressing anger is this: When you choose not to express it, you are doing so because it would not be appropriate under the circumstances, and you leave the situation feeling satisfied that you have made the right choice. When you suppress your anger, you are usually doing it in order to stay in someone's good graces, and you leave the situation with lowered self-esteem because you have sold yourself out.

So, allow yourself to feel your anger without judging or criticizing yourself for it, but if you choose not to express it you must find a way to move *through* and *beyond* it so that it does not create an obstruction. The downside of expressing it may indeed justify keeping it to yourself. Even so, you have some work to do. If you attempt to move *around* it or *ignore* it, it will not go away. You can move through it silently by acknowledging it to yourself, looking with curiosity at why the situation made you angry and determining any changes you can make to the situation to prevent its recurrence. This involves processing the anger internally rather than externally. It does not mean that you simply tell yourself to "make it go away." During the internal process, you may identify feelings that underlie the anger — hurt, sadness, disappointment and so on — and you may want to think about how you might express those underlying feelings to the other person. Unless you acknowledge the feelings at least to yourself, you will not be able to forgive the people who hurt, saddened, or disappointed you. Refusing to look at the feelings will cause you to keep them locked up inside, and your anger will turn bitter with age.

There may be times when you feel the need to express your anger but it feels too intense. When that happens, it's best to stay on the safe side, concentrate internally on what you are feeling, and calm down before you say anything. Intense anger fuels aggressive reaction. One of the factors that can affect the intensity of your anger is your emotional state at the time. For example, if you are already feeling stressed out, or if you are tired, you are more likely to feel anger more intensely if something irritates you. Stress and fatigue can be "red flags" that let you know that you are susceptible to handling anger poorly. Different people have different red flags. It is helpful to be aware of your own particular red flags so that you can anticipate potential trouble spots and prepare yourself to manage them if they arise. Sometimes these red flags are physical feelings, such as quickened heart rate or sweating. If you become conscious of the signs that tell you that you're getting angry, you can take steps to prevent your anger from escalating into aggression. Being able to read your own signs of anger is like knowing how to read the clouds to see if a storm is coming.

So now you're aware of some of the sensations that occur when you're getting angry. It's important to identify who or what is the source of your anger. Rather than lashing out at the closest person, take a moment to reflect about why you are angry. Only you can identify the source of your anger, because you are the expert on your own feelings. Notice whether you see a pattern of setups. For example, is your anger frequently the result of judging people or interpreting their motives negatively? If you are reaching conclusions that are not based on actual evidence, think twice before you say anything. Instead, consider what may be driving your judgments or interpretations. Current circumstances may evoke memories of similar experiences in which you distrusted other people or felt disrespected by them. Perhaps because of past encounters with similar people you hold prejudicial beliefs that affect your interactions with another person. This type of introspection isn't easy. You may discover something about yourself that is uncomfortable to look at. Yet, it's another step in managing your anger, another step to getting to its source.

ANGER POINTS

- **A**lways allow yourself to feel your anger.

- **N**ot expressing your anger is different from suppressing it.

- **G**ive yourself time to calm down before expressing your anger.

- **E**motional state affects intensity of anger.

- **R**ed flags enable you to recognize your anger and anticipate potential pitfalls.

14

Angerspeak

You're not always going to decide to process your anger internally and move through it on your own. You need the ability to express your anger when it is appropriate to do so. Doing so helps to preserve your self-esteem. Without the ability to express how a situation affects you, you feel weak and vulnerable. As an analogy, when a body is weak and vulnerable, it becomes sensitive to the slightest nudge. When you are emotionally weak and vulnerable, you become sensitive to the slightest indiscretion of others. The ability to express anger strengthens you emotionally. The most important tactic is to stay conscious about *how* you express it. Healthy anger requires management.

Once you decide to express your anger, you are faced with another choice: (1) to state directly how you feel and why [recommended], or (2) to fly into uncontrolled rage at everyone and everything around you [not recommended]. In making this choice, you may want to consider that uncontrolled displays of anger lead to violence, and nobody wins when anger becomes violent. The emotional wounding that results can do long-lasting damage to a relationship. Any type of out-of-control expressions and displays of anger are unhealthy and will not produce the results you are seeking. When you express anger without control, your targets often have little to do with the cause of the anger. It is essential to learn to manage your anger — to put it on a leash, as the title of this book suggests — in order to use it effectively. If you express your anger in a healthy way, you'll find that it will disappear once it has served its purpose. That purpose may be merely letting the other person know how his behavior has affected you. Its purpose may also be to bring about a needed change. These purposes are thwarted in the face of destructive anger.

When you feel ready to express your anger, PAUSE and take a few deep breaths. Count to ten. Notice where in your body you may be carrying your anger and breathe into that place. The key is to express your anger assertively and calmly, rather than aggressively. When you speak your anger effectively, you are more likely to be heard and get more of what you need. Be sure that your degree of anger appropriately matches the situation. If the situation is slightly upsetting, don't respond in the same way as you would to a situation that infuriates you.

If you feel as though you have your anger under control, it's time to let the other person know how you feel. When you finally do express your anger, stick to "I" statements as much as you can. "I" statements enable you to state directly how you feel and are less likely to evoke defensiveness in the other person. As soon as you use a "you" statement, the other person feels attacked and becomes defensive. Her wall will go up, and it's unlikely that she will be willing to listen to anything you say. When you use "I" statements, you talk about your own experience. Because her wall is down, she is open to hearing, listening and responding to what you are saying.

How to Do "I" Statements

Suppose you feel angry over something that someone has done. It's a good idea to follow particular phrasing when composing your "I" statements. This is especially so when you are just learning to express your feelings or when you are trying to change the way you have been expressing them up to this point. The formula is:

"I feel _____ A _____ when you _____ B _____ because _____ C _____."

Do you remember high school math classes where you were given a formula to help you solve a problem? If you used the wrong numbers in the formula, you didn't get the desired results. Just as in high school math class, learning the formula for "I" statements is only half the task. In order to make the formula work, you must fill in the blanks with appropriate terms. So, here's the key to the formula:

A = a *feeling* word. Be sure it *is* a feeling word, and not a thought. Here's a list of feeling words to describe your unpleasant emotions. I've organized them into what I call "feeling families."

AFRAID	**ANGRY**	**CONFUSED**	**DEPRESSED**
Alarmed	Annoyed	Disillusioned	Ashamed
Anxious	Bitter	Embarrassed	Disapointed
Doubtful	Enraged	Hesitant	Guilty
Fearful	Furious	Indecisive	Lousy
Nervous	Incensed	Lost	Miserable
Panicky	Provoked	Perplexed	Powerless
Restless	Resentful	Skeptical	Sulky
Scared	Sore	Uncertain	Terrible
Terrified	Upset		
Wary			

HELPLESS	**HURT**	**INDIFFERENT**	**SAD**
Alone	Alienated	Bored	Blue
Distressed	Crushed	Cold	Depressed
Empty	Dejected	Disinterested	Grieved
Frustrated	Heartbroken	Insensitive	Hurt
Incapable	Injured	Lifeless	Lonely
Paralyzed	Offended	Preoccupied	Pessimistic
Useless	Pained	Reserved	Tearful
Vulnerable	Rejected	Weary	Unhappy
	Tormented		
	Victimized		

There are two words that will signal that you are using thought statements instead of feeling statements: "like" and "that." Although it may sound to you as though you are using a feeling statement, if you use the word "like" or "that" immediately after the word "feel," you are not expressing a feeling; you are expressing a thought. For example, "I feel *like* you're not understanding me" and "I feel *that* you don't understand me" are thoughts. Thoughts often contain judgments. Before you know it, you'll be arguing about whether or not the other person understands you. "I feel misunderstood" is a feeling statement. Notice that when you open by expressing a feeling you don't use the dreaded "you" word. You are not accusing the other person of misunderstanding you; you are merely stating how you *feel*. Consequently, the other person remains open to what you are saying.

B = an *objective* statement of what the other person is saying or doing that makes you feel A. Refrain from the temptation to interpret or judge, and rather imagine that you are a newspaper reporter reporting the words or actions without bias. For example, if you feel hurt because your partner has called you lazy, an objective non-judgmental statement would be, "I feel frustrated when you say I'm lazy because I try to help as much as I can, but I run out of time and can't always finish some of the household chores." Or, if it bothers you when your partner goes out and doesn't give you an estimated time of return, you might say, "I feel anxious when you leave without telling me when you'll be back because it makes it difficult for me to plan my own day." In either example, you are objectively describing what makes you feel the way you feel. Because you are not judging or interpreting, you keep the focus on your feeling, where you want it to be. If, on the other hand, you say "I feel frustrated when you try to push my buttons by calling me lazy" or "I feel anxious when you don't care enough about me to let me know when you'll be back," you are interpreting the other person's behavior. He will feel accused and the discussion and argument will shift to whether or not your interpretation is correct.

C = an explanation of the reason you feel A when the other person does B. Again, stay away from interpretations and judgments, and speak only of your own experience. For example, "...because you never think about me" is a judgment. You will end up arguing about how frequently the other person thinks about you, and your attempt to express yourself will get sidetracked. If you say, "...because I make an effort to let you know when I'll be back," you're keeping the focus on the reason you're feeling A.

Learning the formula and using it effectively takes a lot of practice. It's like learning a new language — the language of anger. In an ideal world, the "I" statement will open doors to constructive conversation. But as you try to use this new form of communication, be mindful that it may be significantly different from your usual way of communicating. Unless your partner, child, friend or co-worker has also read this book, the first few times you speak in "I" statements, she may react oddly or regard you with some suspicion. Don't let that derail your efforts. It may be to your advantage to own up to the people in your life that you are trying something new. Maybe you can explain how "I" statements are done so that they can try them.

As with any new language, communicating differently can open up avenues of communication that you never thought possible. The advantage of expressing yourself in this way is that it enables you to stay current with your feelings, and prevents you from harboring anger until it must explode.

To guide you in practicing your own "I" statements, I've included some sample conversations in the Appendix, along with a wallet-size list of the feeling words presented above. Take a look at the examples, cut the list out and carry it with you. It may come in handy as you begin to work on identifying your feelings.

Body language
Take a look at yourself in a mirror when you feel angry.

Anger: Let the Tiger Out, But Keep It on a Leash

This may be a dimension of your anger that you've never considered before now. Notice your posture. Do you make yourself look large and intimidating, as if you're poised to attack, or are you standing up straight, with your shoulders back? What's your facial expression? Is your forehead or jaw tense, or do you look relatively calm?

If you are developing a working relationship with your anger, it's important to see how you look when you feel angry. After all, this is how others are seeing you.

ANGER POINTS

- **A**n ability to express anger effectively strengthens you emotionally.

- **N**ot being in control of your anger will keep you from achieving desired results.

- **G**o to your "I feel…" formula to express your anger and underlying feelings.

- **E**xplosions of pent-up anger are avoided when you stay current with your feelings.

- **R**eworking your anger patterns includes awareness of body language.

15

Oh, the Challenge of Relationships!

I have encouraged you to become aware of the physical signs that accompany your anger. In the same way, look for your partner's physical signs of anger: taut muscles, sweating, trembling, face flushing and so on. When you notice one of these signs, mirror back to your partner verbally what it is that you see — for example, "You seem tense." Responding to his anger with empathy rather than defensiveness can enable the two of you to discuss the situation calmly.

You may not have learned as a child that anger plays an ordinary and important function in any healthy, affectionate relationship. As a child you may have learned to suppress your anger altogether for fear of getting punished or being disliked. The risk with that approach is that your anger did not go anywhere. You may have harbored it inside and it "came out sideways," sometimes erupting like a volcano when the people around you least expected it and in a way that you could not control. If you never had an opportunity to look at your anger, you brought what you learned into your adult relationships.

Whenever you share living quarters with at least one other person, it is inevitable that you will feel angry toward them from time to time. A red flag goes up for me when couples tell me they never fight. They declare this as if it were a major accomplishment. It tells me they are probably evading something. They are either emulating what they were taught as children in terms of avoiding conflict or they are attempting to avoid the type of conflict that *was* present in their childhood families. These couples learn through exercises how to do the things you have been reading about in this book: to identify the source of their anger, to allow themselves to express it, and to resolve problems together. This training in how to handle conflict helps to dispel any idealistic dreams a couple may have that they will always agree on everything and to conquer the anxiety that causes them to stay away from confrontation at all costs.

Time-Outs

One of the most important tools you can use as a couple when either of you is angry is the time-out — a temporary, respectful withdrawal from a situation that may get out of hand. Depending on your experience as a child, the concept of "time out" may seem like a form of punishment in that it may have felt isolating to you when you were a child. Couple time-outs are not meant to be punitive but are a means of taking care of yourself in a potentially escalating situation. Time-outs do not solve the problem at hand but do enable you to take a step back, calm down, and then return to your partner at a *pre-agreed time* to seek resolution calmly. If you familiarize yourself with a time-out "script" like this, you will be prepared to use it when the need arises:

"I'm feeling too upset to continue this discussion right now, and I don't want to say something I don't mean. I'm going to take a time-out and _____ (go out for a walk, for example). I'll be back in _____ (an hour, for example) and I'd like to try talking about this again when I get back."

You can fill in the blanks with whatever activity you choose to help you calm down and however long you need to do it. Providing this information to your partner will prevent her from feeling abandoned or rejected while you are gone. If you get stuck in traffic and cannot make it back in time, *call.*

You must make contact when you said you would; otherwise, the time-out will lose its effectiveness as a tool. While you are on your time-out, refrain from ruminating about what just happened, playing the tape over and over in your head. This will only fuel your anger and defeat the purpose of the time-out. Instead, talk to yourself calmly, as you would to a child who is upset and needs comforting. After all, there is probably a hurt child within you whose feelings need to be acknowledged. Try to do something physical to work off the tension you are feeling. Go for a walk or exercise at the gym. (Although I don't advocate it myself, some therapists advise their clients to vent their anger by punching a pillow or a punching bag. They view this as a catharsis. However, some studies have shown that venting anger in this way escalates anger rather than dissipating it.) When you reunite with your partner, you can continue the discussion, agree to postpone it to a specific day and time that you mutually agree on, or maybe even decide to drop the issue because you both agree that it was petty, after all. Again, if you postpone the discussion, it's important to set a specific time to revisit it so that it doesn't get put off indefinitely and never get addressed.

Experimenting

If you and your partner are not accustomed to expressing anger, it may be helpful to agree to experiment with expressing your feelings, including anger, in a safe setting. Think of it as a sort of "laboratory." One way to do this is for you to set aside a specific time and place during the week when you both will meet for twenty minutes to communicate about issues important to your relationship. Alternate the roles of listener and speaker. When you are the speaker, your task is to express your feelings using "I feel" statements (see Chapter 14). You must do this in a way that is honest and direct, yet respectful of your partner. This is not a time to unload on your partner with a barrage of verbal attacks. When you have communicated your feelings in two or three sentences, switch roles. Now you become the listener. As listener, your job is simply to listen. You may not interrupt or react in any way. Refrain from using body language such as rolling your eyes, or nonverbal sounds such as sighing. Remember, you and your partner are trying to create a safe environment in which you can learn how to communicate more effectively. Any reaction while your partner speaks will serve only to discourage him from practicing with you in the future.

Rupture and Repair

If your past experience with anger has resulted in rejection or the ending of relationships, you may think of anger as a severance. Thinking of it in this way would probably make you want to avoid it. See if you can begin to think of anger as merely a "rupture." Then, the ensuing communication becomes an effort to "repair." The focus of your couples experiment can be "rupture and repair." This can be an eye opener if you have never considered that you can feel both anger and affection for your partner at the same time. Actually, anger frequently comes when you *do* feel love for the other person. The fact that you feel upset can itself be evidence that you care about your partner and about the relationship. Suppose your partner works late but didn't call to let you know. You get concerned and worried that something has happened to her. When she finally walks through the door you express anger, but the real source of your anger is your concern for her safety and anxiety over what may have happened. It is possible for you to feel anger in one moment, express it, and then express the affection that was also there all the while. In a relationship, expressing anger may create a rupture, but the ability to receive it, accept it and address its cause repairs the rupture.

Although anger is unpleasant, it doesn't have to polarize partners. If you can accept the expression of your partner's anger, the situation becomes shared and something the two of you can work together to resolve. As the anger cools down and you move into problem-solving mode, you become teammates.

Your affection for each other can strengthen when you express your anger effectively. However, if anger goes unexpressed, it is difficult for you to feel close to your partner. Your affection for each other is numbed by the pent-up anger. When couples say that they have lost their attraction to each other, it's usually the case that unexpressed anger has come between them. It may not even be that they are angry at *each other.* They might be angry with someone or something else. Rather than directing the anger at its source and expressing these negative feelings openly, they suppress them. Angry people cannot be responsive, affectionate partners. The air needs to be cleared so that communication and warmth may flow.

ANGER POINTS

- **A**wareness of your partner's physical signs of anger enables you to be ready with empathy.

- **N**ever fighting does not necessarily mean your relationship is free of problems.

- **G**iving yourself a time-out is a way of avoiding a potentially escalating situation.

- **E**xperiment with how it feels to give and take anger.

- **R**upture-and-repair can replace the idea that anger results in severance.

16

A Parent's Refrain: I Never Thought I Would Feel Like This!

Let's be honest. Parenting is not an easy job. Parents *do* get angry. Your children may push you to the point where you feel you have reached the last straw. It's important for you to acknowledge your feelings and take time for yourself. It is also healthy for your children to hear you express frustration or anger and to see you give yourself "time-outs." After all, your children model their behavior after yours.

If you feel angry with your child, consider why you are angry. Are you really angry because of what he said or did, or because you are concerned about what friends, relatives or teachers will think if they find out what he said or did? Remind yourself what it was like for you when you were your child's age. It helps to put it all in perspective.

There are times when you *will* want to express your anger at your child. Do it in a way that provides role modeling for her. The expression of anger is healthy and should be taught. But you have control over how you display your anger and the manner in which you choose to express it. If you model your anger well, your child will learn how to express her own anger and needs effectively. While the feeling of anger is natural, how a child reacts to feeling angry is actually a learned behavior.

Suppose the circumstances warrant expressing your anger over something your child has done. Let's look at your choices. You can state that you feel angry and let him know that his behavior has affected you, or you can say nothing, or you can react in a way that's out of control. If you strive to be the "Good Mommy" or "Good Daddy," you may choose to say nothing too often. Parents take this route when they feel threatened by their own angry feelings because they don't know how to manage them. They fear what might happen if they allow themselves to express it. Or they fear that they might make their child "feel bad." But is this the example you want to give? Encourage your child to say, "I am angry," by saying it yourself when you are angry. It's a good idea to give a child a non-angry warning in order to stop a behavior. If he does it again, express your anger openly and clearly. Don't beat around the bush. Tell him that you are angry that he has continued the behavior after you asked him to stop. Tell him what the consequences will be if the behavior continues and follow through on your word if the unwanted behavior persists. Time-outs or the removal of privileges are effective consequences for misbehavior.

When your anger gets out of control, you fail to maintain your child's respect. "Out of control" means any behavior that is used other than directly expressing anger to a child in a way that acknowledges your feeling while also respecting the child. When you give your child the "cold shoulder" or explode with rage, you are teaching her that it's okay to act out when she is angry. Acting out your anger can destroy the relationship between you and your child.

Crying is a common way for children to express their anger, but it does not have to be the only way. You can let your child know there are other ways he can express his anger. Give your young child some guidance by providing tools to enable him to feel his anger and channel it into non-destructive activities. Provide Playdoh to work with his hands, or pillows, stuffed animals, or paper bags to shout into. You may also ask him to draw you a picture to show you how angry he is. Encourage him to imagine what his anger looks like, what color it is, and so on. What's important is that you provide him with a place and the means to articulate his anger, verbally or non-verbally. There should be two rules: He can't hurt himself or anyone else, either physically or emotionally, and he can't deliberately damage anything. Whatever you choose to offer to your child, there's one caveat: Once you offer a particular tool, be prepared to tolerate what it looks or sounds like! The more accustomed you grow to expressing your own anger, the more you will be able to witness and tolerate your child's. When your child expresses his anger in a constructive way, reward his efforts with positive attention, no matter how old he is.

Finally, if you are angry with your partner, assume that your child is listening, and model expressions of anger accordingly. When a child grows up hearing one parent abusing the other — physically, verbally or emotionally — she internalizes the aggression and begins to use it on the people in her own life when she is angry. Children who are regularly exposed to unhealthy anger frequently grow to be adults who express their anger inappropriately at their partners, their children, their friends and the people they work with.

ANGER POINTS

- **A**ll parents get angry.

- **N**otice what is making you angry.

- **G**ive your child positive modeling of how to express anger.

- **E**vading anger or the imposition of consequences for unwanted behavior doesn't help your child.

- **R**espect is lost when you display out-of-control behaviors to your child.

17

You Can Do It!

If you grew up in a family where unhealthy anger was regularly displayed, fortunately all is not lost. Behaviors that are learned can also be unlearned. The challenge for you now that you're an adult will be to unlearn those old behaviors that you realize no longer serve you and learn for the first time how to cope with your anger in a healthier way.

Learning to express your anger effectively involves working on your assertiveness skills. When you are assertive, you honor your own feelings and respect those of the other person. If you have tended to be passive, aggressive, or passive-aggressive in the past, developing assertiveness will take time and practice. Your first attempts will be awkward, and you may be tempted to give up. Keep trying.

Find ways to relax from the stressful life you are living. You may feel as though you can't afford to take the time or spend the money on something as "frivolous" as relaxation. Actually, you can't afford not to. Your stress is directly related to the anger you carry in your body or express outwardly. Look into yoga or meditation, find a massage therapist you like, or once in a while just allow yourself to do nothing for an entire afternoon. If it sounds like a luxury, then you're overdue.

Pay attention to the content of media that you let into your home. Observing aggression in movies, on television, and at sporting events intensifies your own hostility. It seems logical that the more violence you witness the more desensitized you become to it and the lower the bar gets in terms of your own behavior when you yourself feel angry.

Anger is a powerful emotion. Unless you recognize its strength and own your anger, when you encounter it in yourself or others you will feel knocked off your center and at a loss as to how to deal with it. You'll know that you have acquired healthy anger skills when you become angry, are able to focus on what you are feeling, express it respectfully, and genuinely feel good about how you handled a situation.

We are all works in progress. Give yourself credit for even picking up this book and reading it. Be compassionate with yourself as you try to hone your skills. You will no doubt make mistakes along the way. That's part of the learning process.

This book is only a beginning. In addition to the materials in the annotated bibliography/resource list at the end of this book, there are many good therapists worldwide who can help you with anger management and assertiveness skills. Please avail yourself of whatever you think you need to improve your relationships and your life.

Peace.

ANGER POINTS

- Any behavior that was learned can be unlearned.

- Non-assertiveness shows up in either passive, aggressive or passive-aggressive behaviors.

- Give yourself the gift of relaxation.

- Examine the violent content of the media that enters your home.

- Recognize what you need to make the changes you desire, and go for it!

Endnotes

1 This is a universal teaching found in one form or another in the sacred texts of the major religions of the world: Buddhism, Christianity, Confucianism, Hinduism, Islam, Judaism, Taoism, and Zoroastrianism.

2 King Pyrrhus of Epirus conquered the Romans in 279 B.C. but suffered severe casualties. A "Pyrrhic victory" is one that is gained at such great cost that the situation ends up worse than before.

3 Some claim that this is the historical source for the expression "rule of thumb."

4 Men also experience partner abuse, but their reason for remaining silent about it is usually associated with feelings of shame and embarrassment rather than desensitization due to multigenerational patterns.

5 David Wexler, *When Good Men Behave Badly* (Oakland, Calif.: New Harbinger Publications, 2004).

6 Ibid., p. 59-62.

7 Reports indicate that of 69 documented workplace shootings in 2003, people whose employment status had changed unfavorably committed 51.8%. Of these, 23.8% had lost their jobs, and 28% were adversely affected by management decisions in some other way.

8 Researchers have found that anger is a common characteristic of Type A personalities (workaholics).

9 There are many other examples of collective anger in our daily newspapers. Angry community leaders criticize police for shooting unarmed teens. Angry advocates speak out on behalf of victims of hurricane victims. Angry foreign leaders join together to lash at leaders of other countries whose strategies they find distasteful.

10 Stonewalling is emotional unavailability, often accompanied by an empty stare. It leaves a speaker feeling as though he is in fact talking to a stone wall.

Appendix 1

Examples of "I" Statements

Joan: I feel terrible when you tease me about my weight, because I've been trying to lose weight and exercise but haven't had much success.

John: I wasn't aware that it made you feel so bad. I meant it only as good-natured kidding.

Joan: I'm glad I told you how I felt, then.

John: So am I. I'll try to be more conscious of what I say in the future.

Brenda: Mom, I feel stressed when you ask me whether I've found a summer job yet, because I haven't and I'm afraid I won't ever find a place that's looking for someone like me.

Mom: You have seemed worried lately. I won't ask again because I don't want to add to your stress, but I'm here if you need to talk about your job search.

Dad: Bobby, I feel afraid when I see you ride your bike out into the street, because you might get hit by a passing car.

Bobby: Oh, I won't, Daddy. All my friends are allowed to ride their bikes in the street. The cars watch out for us.

Dad: Well, I'm wary of drivers even when I'm driving my car because they can get distracted easily and not pay attention to what they're doing. I'd like you to listen to me on this one. If you got hurt, I'd be very sad.

Bobby: OK, Daddy. I'll stay out of the street.

Appendix 2

Unpleasant Feeling Words

Unpleasant Feeling Words

AFRAID	ANGRY	CONFUSED	DEPRESSED
Alarmed	Annoyed	Disillusioned	Ashamed
Anxious	Bitter	Embarrassed	Disapointed
Doubtful	Enraged	Hesitant	Guilty
Fearful	Furious	Indecisive	Lousy
Nervous	Incensed	Lost	Miserable
Panicky	Provoked	Perplexed	Powerless
Restless	Resentful	Skeptical	Sulky
Scared	Sore	Uncertain	Terrible
Terrified	Upset		
Wary			

HELPLESS	HURT	INDIFFERENT	SAD
Alone	Alienated	Bored	Blue
Distressed	Crushed	Cold	Depressed
Empty	Dejected	Disinterested	Grieved
Frustrated	Heartbroken	Insensitive	Hurt
Incapable	Injured	Lifeless	Lonely
Paralyzed	Offended	Preoccupied	Pessimistic
Useless	Pained	Reserved	Tearful
Vulnerable	Rejected	Weary	Unhappy
	Tormented		
	Victimized		

Appendix 3

Annotated Bibliography/Resource List

Books

Eastman, Meg, and Sydney Craft Rozen. *Taming the Dragon in Your Child: Solutions for Breaking the Cycle of Family Anger.* John Wiley & Sons, 1994. This book seems to have something for everyone. It covers issues encountered by single- and two-parent families of kids from toddlers to teens.

Moser, Adolph. *Don't Fall Apart on Saturdays!: The Children's Divorce-Survival Book.* Landmark Editions, 2000. An excellent explanation of parental divorce for 9- to 12-year-olds.

-----. *Don't Rant & Rave on Wednesdays!: The Children's Anger-Control Book.* Landmark Editions, 1994. This book presents the causes of anger in terms a 4- to 8-year-old child can understand, and shows how children can manage their anger and control their own behavior.

Petracek, Laura J. *The Anger Workbook for Women: How to Keep Your Anger from Undermining Your Self-Esteem, Your Emotional Balance, and Your Relationships.* New Harbinger Publications, 2004. A large-size format that leads you through exercises to enable you to get in touch with your feelings and express them assertively.

Potter-Efron, Ronald, and Patricia S. Potter-Efron. New Harbinger Publications, Inc., 2006. *Letting Go of Anger: The Eleven Most Common Anger Styles &*

What to Do About Them. Shows the problems that
can arise when destructive anger styles are used habit-
ually. Offers practical exercises to help recognize and
change your unhealthy anger patterns.

Prall, Robert C. *The Rights of Children in Separation and
Divorce: The Essential Handbook for Parents.*
Landmark Editions, 2000. Contains practices that parents can follow to help them to act in their children's
best interests while separating or divorcing.

Articles

American Psychological Association. *Controlling Anger –
Before It Controls You.* A clear explanation of anger
and the consequences of different approaches to dealing with this emotion. Online at http://www.apahelp-
center.org/articles/article.php?id=29.

Leopold, Allison. "Anger Management: How to Tame Your
Temper," *Current Health,* November 2004. Written
for middle and high school students, this article dis-
cusses the effect of anger on the body and offers
strategies for anger management. This back issue can
be ordered by phone at 1-800-446-3355 or by e-mail
at customerservice@weeklyreader.com.

SAMHSA's National Mental Health Information Center.
Helping the Child Who Is Expressing Anger. United
States Department of Health and Human Services,
2003. An explanation of what you as a parent can do
to help your angry child. Online at
http://www.mentalhealth.samhsa.gov/publications/
allpubs/Ca-0032/default.asp

"Teen Trouble: Drugs, Sex, Depression: Canadian Experts on
How to Help Kids to Survive Trying Times,"
Maclean's, March 1, 2004. This nine-page cover story
contains wisdom and insight for parents of teenagers
on a variety of topics, including bullying, learning and
behavioral problems, bad friends and anger. This
back issue can be ordered by phone at 1-866-301-
4414.

CD-ROM

Anderson, George. *An Everyday Guide to Anger Management.* eTotal Source, 2002. Psychotherapist and teacher Anderson guides you through an interactive program to show you how to manage anger, control stress and improve relationships. Includes an anger management pocket handbook, an interactive video CD-ROM and a bookmark listing quick tips.

Bosworth, Kris. *SMARTteam: Managing Anger and SMARTteam: Resolving Conflicts.* Learning Multi-Systems, 2003. Designed for kids ages 11 to 15, this software includes guidance in expressing anger and using mediation strategies in situations that are familiar to kids in this age group.

DVD

Elkind + Sweet Communications, *Preventing Conflicts and Violence.* Part of a series of DVD videos entitled *Big Changes Big Choices,* this program contains many tips for young teens on how to prevent conflict from escalating by recognizing their choices and dealing with their anger in non-violent ways.

VHS

Trudeau, Pierre M. (dir.) and Leduc, Yves (prod.) *Kid Stuff/Enfantillage.* National Film Board of Canada, 1990. This six-minute video depicts the effect of parental fighting on a child who overhears the conflict.

Website

Namka, Lynne. *Get Your Angries Out.* Dr. Namka offers substantial information on anger skills for adults, kids, parents, couples and teachers. Online at http://www.angriesout.com/namka.htm

Appendix 4

Words of Wisdom: On Anger

"The anger of lovers renews the strength of love."
> Publius Syrus, *Maxim 24,* c. 42 B.C.

"Fanaticism is to superstition what delirium is to fever, and what rage is to anger."
> Voltaire, *Philosophical Dictionary,*
> "Fanaticism," 1764

"When angry, count ten, before you speak; if very angry, a hundred."
> Thomas Jefferson, *Writings,* 1899

"I was angry with my friend:
I told my wrath, my wrath did end.
I was angry with my foe:
I told it not, my wrath did grow."
> William Blake, *Songs of Experience,*
> "A Poison Tree," 1794

"If you are patient in one moment of anger, you will escape a hundred days of sorrow."
> Chinese Proverb

"Anybody can become angry, that is easy; but to be angry with the right person, and to the right degree, and at the right time, and for the right purpose, and in the right way, that is not within everybody's power and is not easy."

Aristotle, *The Nichomachean Ethics*, c. 340 B.C.

"This at least should be a rule through the letter-writing world: that no angry letter be posted till four-and-twenty hours will have elapsed since it was written."

Anthony Trollope, *The Bertrams*, 1859

"My tongue will tell the anger of mine heart,
Or else my heart, concealing it, will break."

William Shakespeare, *Taming of the Shrew*

"Do not speak harshly to any one; those who are spoken to will answer thee in the same way. Angry speech is painful: blows for blows will touch thee."

The Dhammapada, c. 300 B.C.

Index

Buy additional copies of

"Anger: Let the Tiger Out, But Keep It on a Leash"

Do you wonder what causes your angry feelings? This book will help you to understand the purpose that anger serves in your life. Whether you tend to stuff your anger or explode with it, you will find thought-provoking insight within the pages of this book. You will discover:
- That anger is a natural emotion.
- How your childhood experience of anger has influenced your experience of anger as an adult.
- The importance of allowing yourself to feel your anger.
- How to improve your relationships by expressing your anger in respectful and effective ways.

Mary Ellen Halloran has a Master of Arts degree in Counseling Psychology from the California Institute of Integral Studies in San Francisco. She is a licensed marriage and family therapist with a private practice in San Francisco. She has helped many clients to develop a healthier view of their own anger so that they can manage it more effectively.

This book has enabled many to change their relationships, and it will show you the way to do this, too. Don't wait another day! Use the convenient order form on the other side of this page to order additional copies today.

Timepiece Publishing Company
Personal Development Books and CDs

Order Form

Fax orders: 510-658-4778. Send this form.
Telephone orders: Call 888-812-7437. Have credit card ready.
Postal orders: Timepiece Publishing Co., P.O. Box 3508, Oakland CA 94609, USA. Send this form.

Please print
Name:_____
Address:_____
City:_____ State:_____ Zip:_____
Country:_____
Telephone:_____
E-mail address:_____

Please send _____ copies of Anger: *Let the Tiger Out, But Keep It on a Leash* **at $12.95 each plus shipping**

Quantity _____ x $12.95 each = $ _____

Shipping
USA: $4 for first book, $2 each add'l book   _____
Int'l: $9 for first book, $5 each add'l book   _____

California residents add 8.75% sales tax   _____

Total Amount Due $ _____

Payment type
_____ Check enclosed, payable to Timepiece Publishing Co.
___ Visa ___ MasterCard ___ AMEX ___ Discover
Card number:_____
Name on card:_____ Exp. Date: _____
Signature: _____ Date: _____

All prices are in U.S. dollars. Orders must be prepaid. Personal checks drawn on U.S. banks, money orders, VISA, MasterCard and American Express are all accepted. All credit card orders must include a billing/shipping address, card expiration date, daytime phone number, and signature.